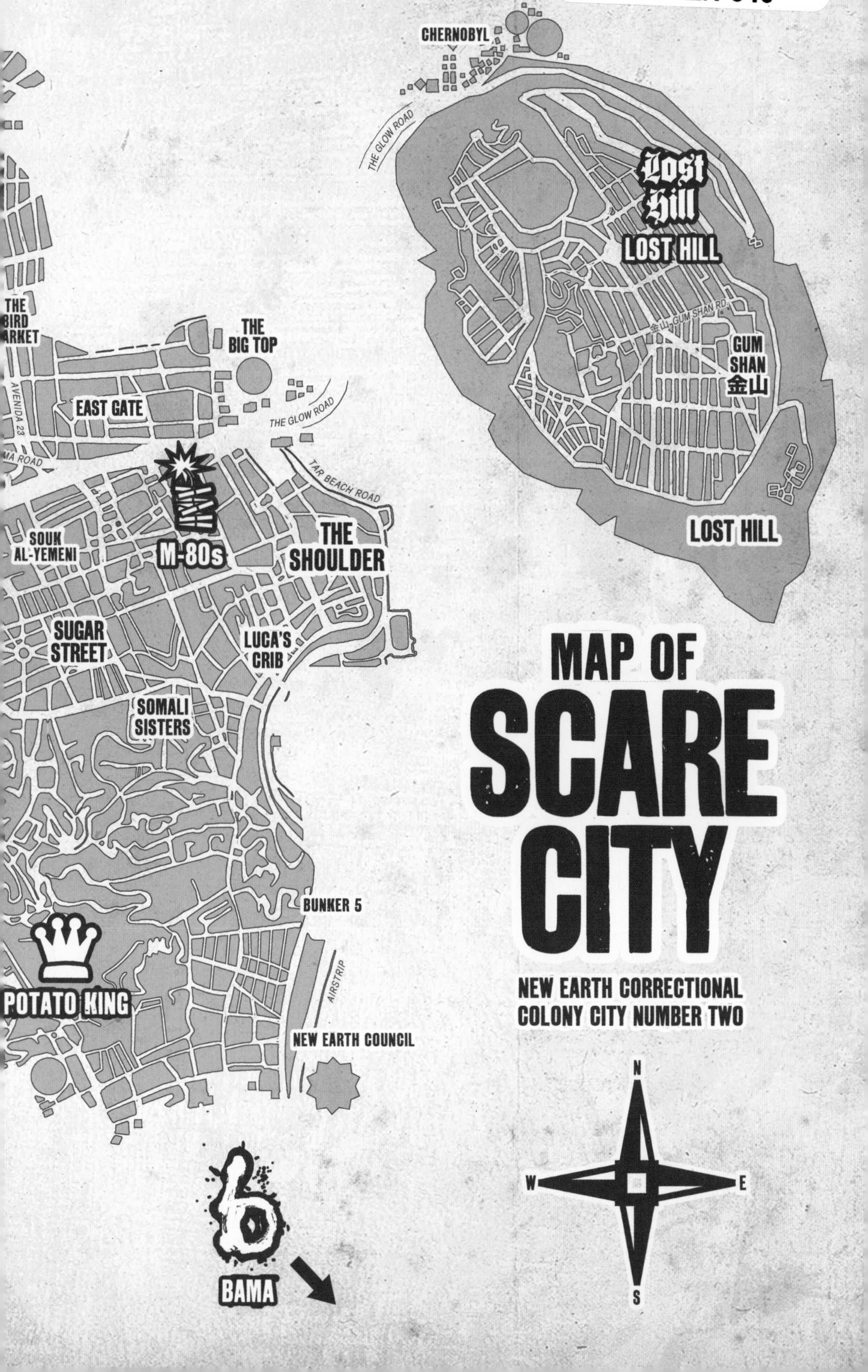
CHERNOBYL
THE GLOW ROAD
Lost Hill
LOST HILL
金山 GUM SHAN RD.
GUM
SHAN
金山
LOST HILL
THE
BIRD
ARKET
THE
BIG TOP
AVENIDA 23
EAST GATE
THE GLOW ROAD
MA ROAD
TAR BEACH ROAD
SOUK
AL-YEMENI
M-80s
THE
SHOULDER
SUGAR
STREET
LUCA'S
CRIB
SOMALI
SISTERS
MAP OF
SCARE
CITY
NEW EARTH CORRECTIONAL
COLONY CITY NUMBER TWO
BUNKER 5
AIRSTRIP
POTATO KING
NEW EARTH COUNCIL
N
W
E
S
BAMA

CONCRETE PARK

VOLUME 1: YOU SEND ME

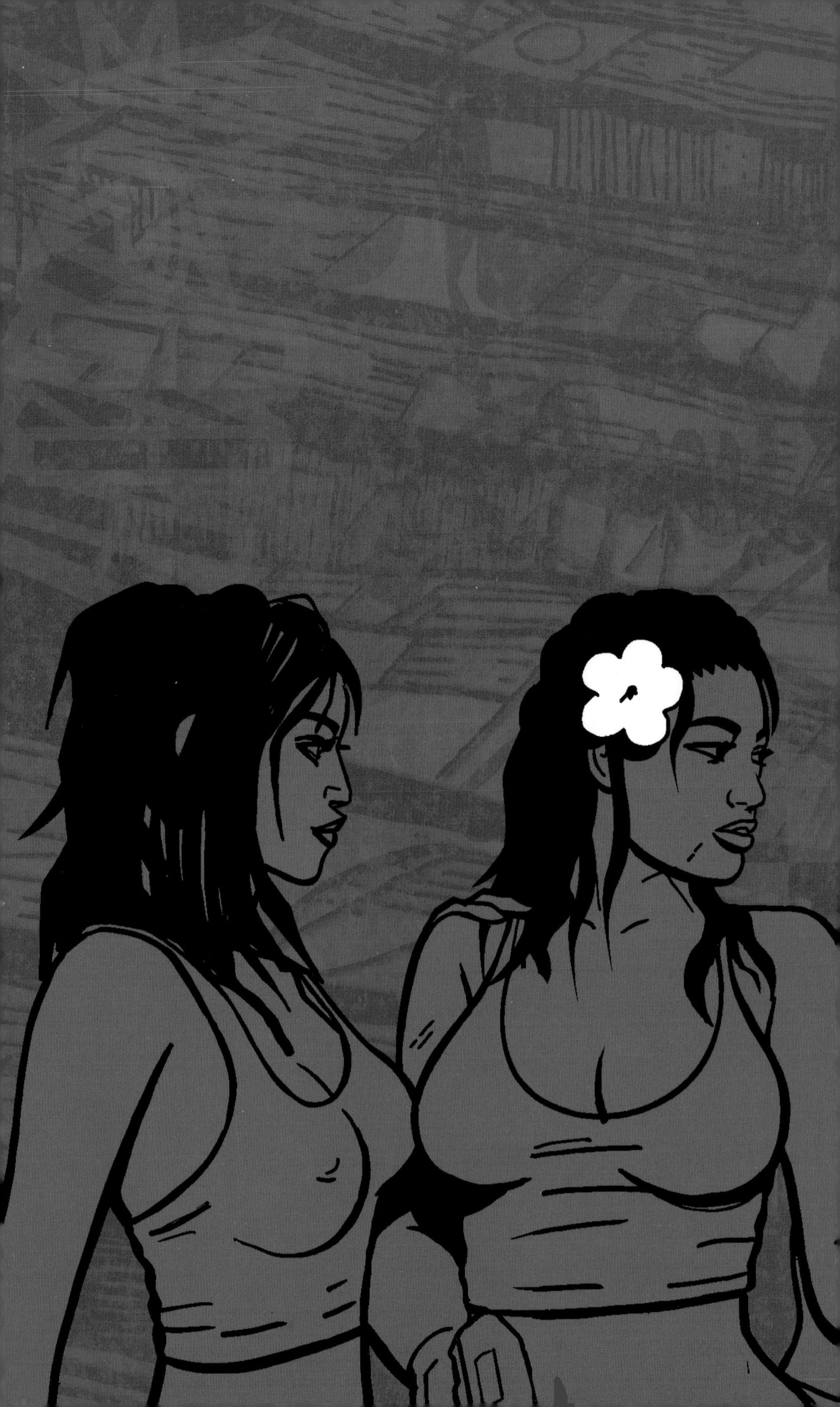

CONCRETE PARK™

VOLUME 1: YOU SEND ME

CREATED BY
**TONY PURYEAR, ERIKA ALEXANDER,
AND ROBERT ALEXANDER**

WRITTEN BY
TONY PURYEAR AND ERIKA ALEXANDER

ARTWORK, COLORS,
AND LETTERS BY
TONY PURYEAR

TEAM CONCRETE PARK
COLOR ASSISTANT: ALICIA BURSTEIN
COLOR ASSISTANT: ALEXANDRA QUINBY
LEGAL: LICHTER, GROSSMAN, NICHOLS,
ADLER & FELDMAN, INC.

3D VEHICLE MODEL "WEAZEL" BY CHRIS "DZFIRE" LOCKE.
3D MECH MODEL "BE02K10" BY MESTOPHALES.

VISIT CONCRETEPARK.COM

DARK HORSE BOOKS

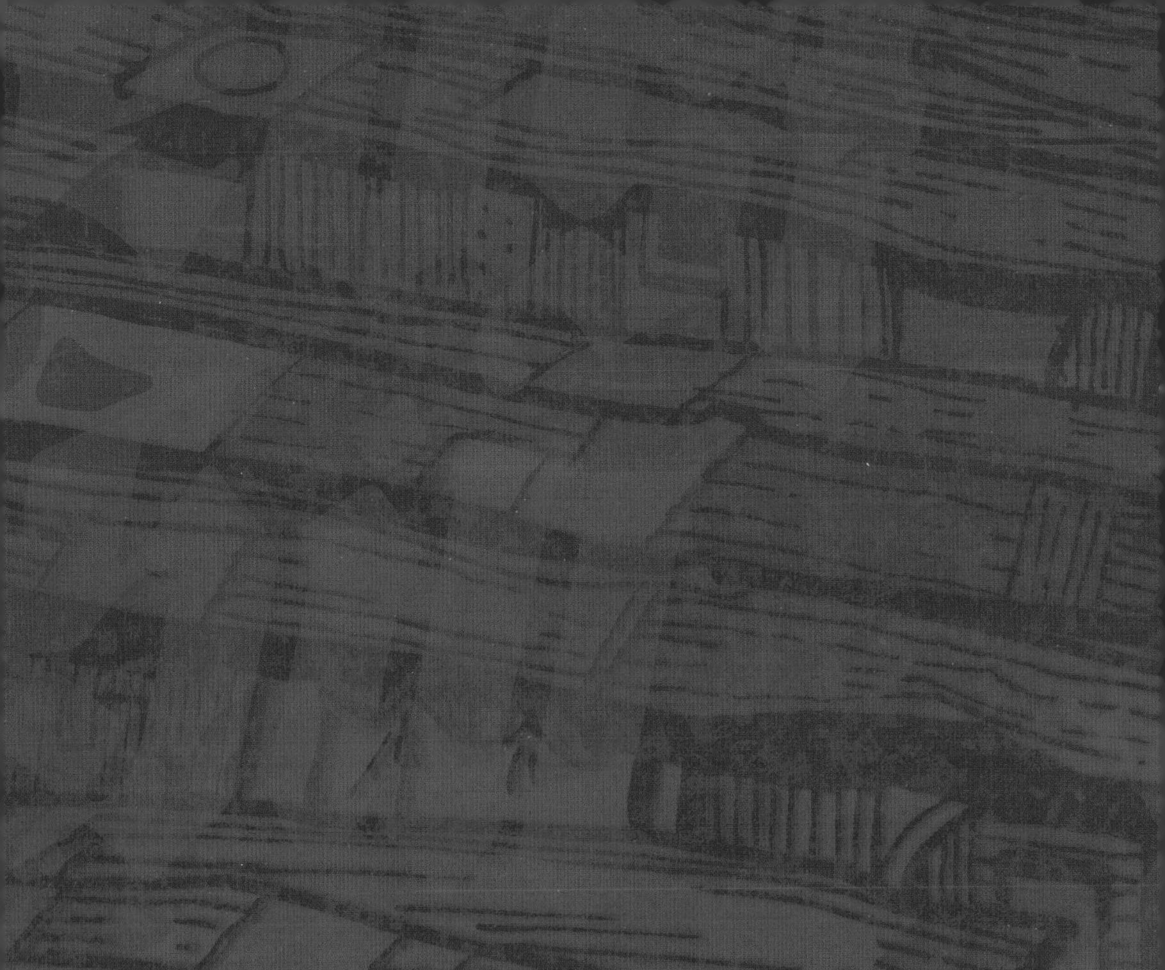

Publisher . . . . **MIKE RICHARDSON**

Editor . . . . **PHILIP R. SIMON**

Assistant Editor . . . . **ROXY POLK**

Designer . . . . **NICK JAMES**

Digital Production . . . . **CHRISTINA McKENZIE**

CONCRETE PARK VOLUME 1: YOU SEND ME

Text and illustrations of Concrete Park™ © 2011, 2012, 2014 Concrete Park, Inc. All other material, unless otherwise specified, is © 2014 Dark Horse Comics, Inc. Dark Horse Books® and the Dark Horse logo are registered trademarks of Dark Horse Comics, Inc. All rights reserved. No portion of this publication may be reproduced or transmitted, in any form or by any means, without the express written permission of Dark Horse Comics, Inc. Names, characters, places, and incidents featured in this publication either are the product of the author's imagination or are used fictitiously. Any resemblance to actual persons (living or dead), events, institutions, or locales, without satiric intent, is coincidental.

CONCRETE PARK: YOU SEND ME ORIGINALLY APPEARED IN *DARK HORSE PRESENTS* #7 THROUGH #9 AND #14 THROUGH #17, PUBLISHED IN 2011 AND 2012, AND HAS BEEN REVISED AND EXPANDED FOR THIS COLLECTION.

PUBLISHED BY
DARK HORSE BOOKS
A DIVISION OF DARK HORSE COMICS, INC.
10956 SE MAIN STREET
MILWAUKIE, OR 97222

DARKHORSE.COM | CONCRETEPARK.COM

TO FIND A COMICS SHOP IN YOUR AREA, CALL THE COMIC SHOP LOCATOR SERVICE TOLL-FREE AT 1-888-266-4226.

FIRST EDITION: OCTOBER 2014
ISBN 978-1-61655-530-6

10 9 8 7 6 5 4 3 2 1

PRINTED IN CHINA

MIKE RICHARDSON PRESIDENT AND PUBLISHER • **NEIL HANKERSON** EXECUTIVE VICE PRESIDENT • **TOM WEDDLE** CHIEF FINANCIAL OFFICER • **RANDY STRADLEY** VICE PRESIDENT OF PUBLISHING • **MICHAEL MARTENS** VICE PRESIDENT OF BOOK TRADE SALES • **ANITA NELSON** VICE PRESIDENT OF BUSINESS AFFAIRS • **SCOTT ALLIE** EDITOR IN CHIEF • **MATT PARKINSON** VICE PRESIDENT OF MARKETING • **DAVID SCROGGY** VICE PRESIDENT OF PRODUCT DEVELOPMENT • **DALE LaFOUNTAIN** VICE PRESIDENT OF INFORMATION TECHNOLOGY • **DARLENE VOGEL** SENIOR DIRECTOR OF PRINT, DESIGN, AND PRODUCTION • **KEN LIZZI** GENERAL COUNSEL • **DAVEY ESTRADA** EDITORIAL DIRECTOR • **CHRIS WARNER** SENIOR BOOKS EDITOR • **DIANA SCHUTZ** EXECUTIVE EDITOR • **CARY GRAZZINI** DIRECTOR OF PRINT AND DEVELOPMENT • **LIA RIBACCHI** ART DIRECTOR • **CARA NIECE** DIRECTOR OF SCHEDULING • **MARK BERNARDI** DIRECTOR OF DIGITAL PUBLISHING

TONY PURYEAR

Thanks to my two amazing co-creators, Erika Alexander and Robert Alexander, for the world and the fun and the struggle. Thanks to my parents, Leon and Dorothy Puryear, for loving every drawing I ever did— but insisting I try harder. Thanks to Lesley, my supportive sister. Thanks to the Zhang family of Shanghai and New York for believing in us. Thanks to Peter Nichols, the best entertainment lawyer in the game and my attorney of twenty years. Thanks to Mike Richardson, the gutsiest publisher in comics—and the nicest. Thanks to Philip Simon, a prince among editors. Thanks, Jim Gibbons. Thanks to the hard-working team at Dark Horse Comics. Thanks to Dan Farr for years of support and love. Thanks to Alicia Burstein and Daniel Presedo. Thanks to Alexandra Quinby. Thanks, again, and love to Erika, for making the world so beautiful.

ERIKA ALEXANDER

Thank you, Sammie "Mom" Alexander, my inspiration. Thanks to my talented brother Robert Alexander, the Alexander family, Jennifer Levine, Jeff Bernstein, Greene & Associates, Michael Hermann, and Doris and Val at Samy's Camera. Thanks to Jeff Smith, guest editor of *Best American Comics 2013*. Thanks to my friend and mentor, Hillary Clinton. Thanks to all my Facebook friends for love, encouragement, and vodka. My deepest thanks and love to Tony Puryear, resident boy genius.

ROBERT ALEXANDER

Thanks to Dyan, Erika, our families, and the visionary who made it all happen . . . Tony Puryear.

"The past is painful,
 the present, precarious,
 but the future . . .
 the future is free."
 —Chavez

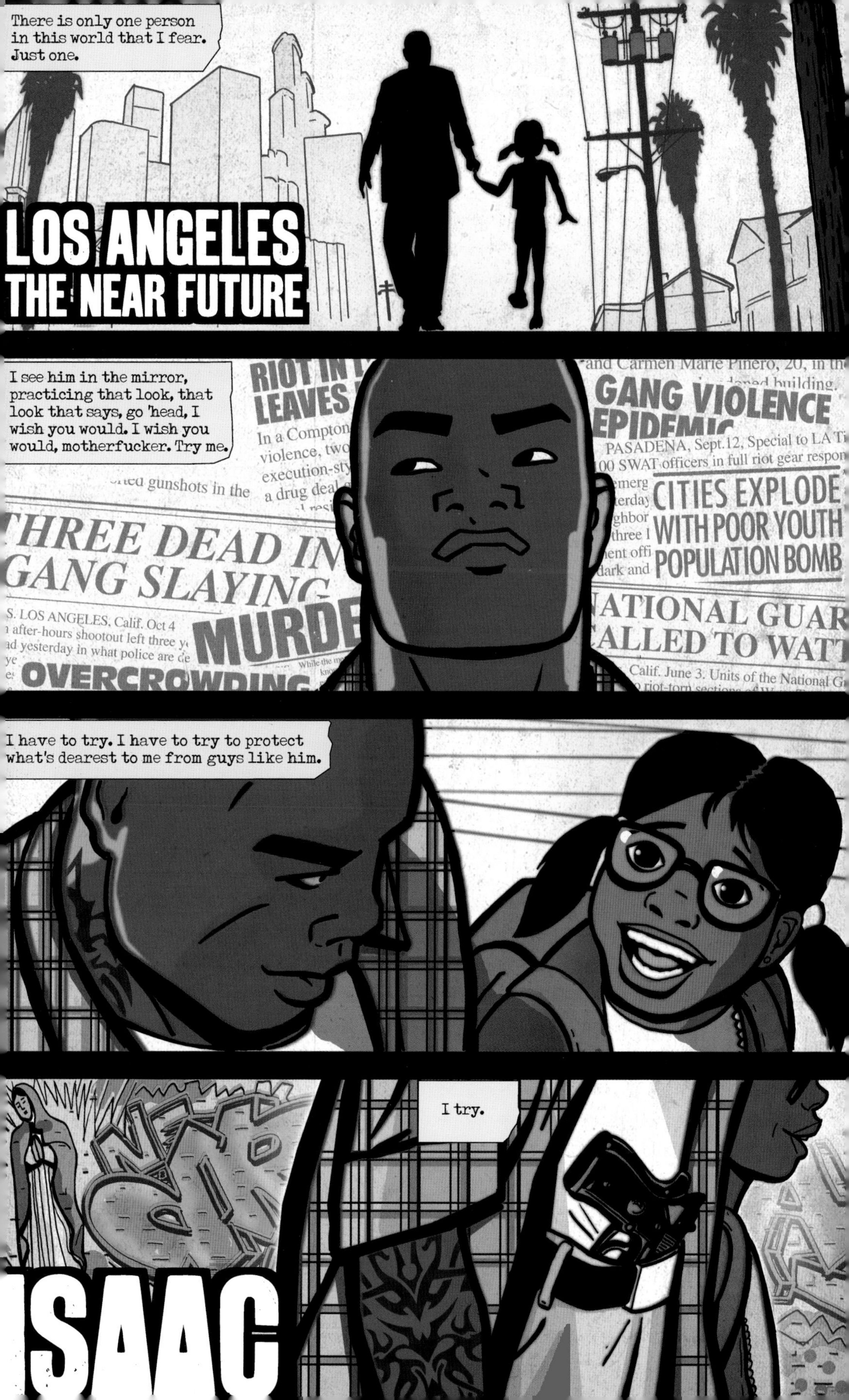
There is only one person in this world that I fear. Just one.
LOS ANGELES
THE NEAR FUTURE
I see him in the mirror, practicing that look, that look that says, go 'head, I wish you would. I wish you would, motherfucker. Try me.
GANG VIOLENCE
CITIES EXPLODE
WITH POOR YOUTH
POPULATION BOMB
I have to try. I have to try to protect what's dearest to me from guys like him.
I try.
ISAAC

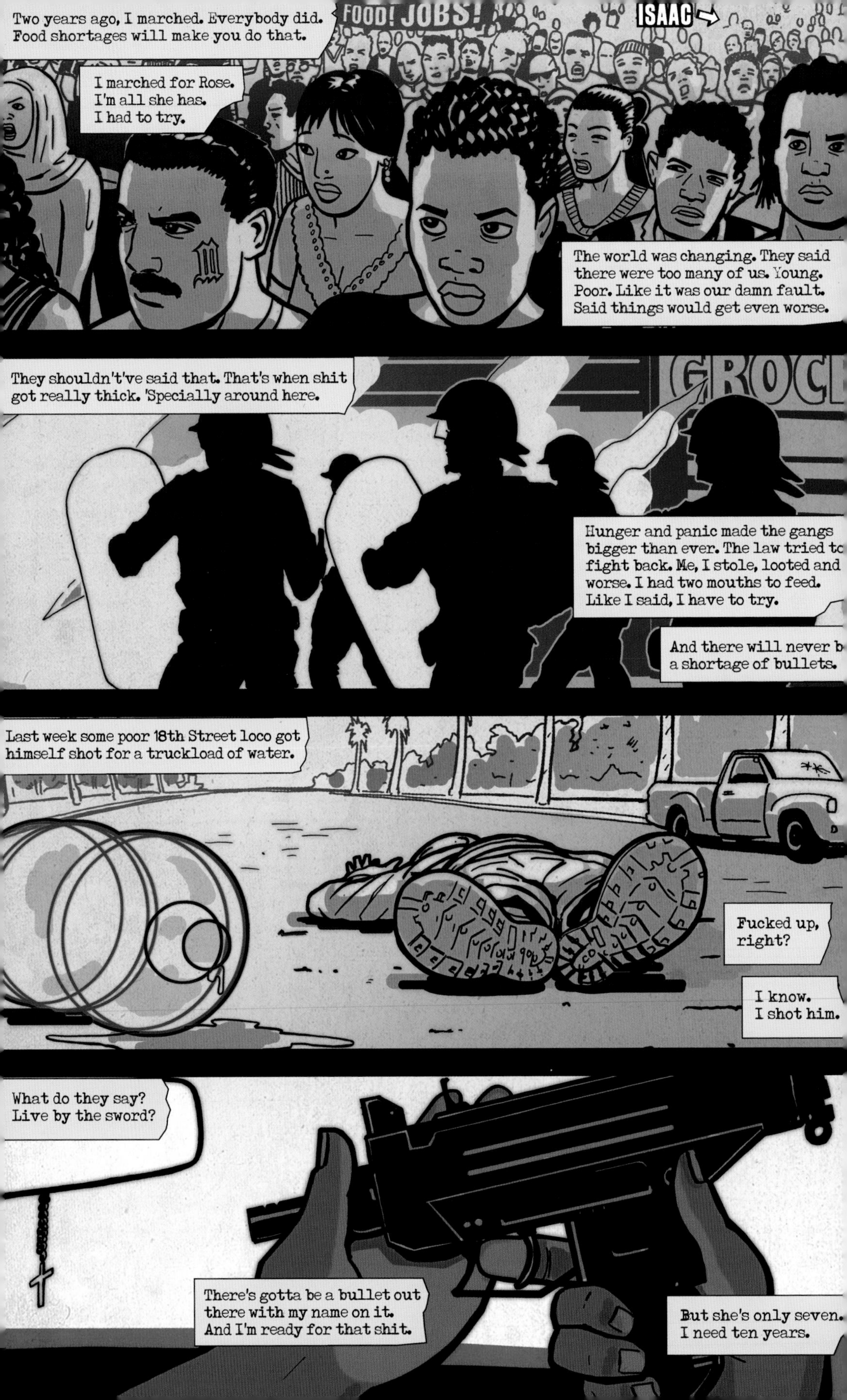
Two years ago, I marched. Everybody did. Food shortages will make you do that.
FOOD! JOBS!
ISAAC
I marched for Rose. I'm all she has. I had to try.
The world was changing. They said there were too many of us. Young. Poor. Like it was our damn fault. Said things would get even worse.
They shouldn't've said that. That's when shit got really thick. 'Specially around here.
GROC
Hunger and panic made the gangs bigger than ever. The law tried to fight back. Me, I stole, looted and worse. I had two mouths to feed. Like I said, I have to try.
And there will never be a shortage of bullets.
Last week some poor 18th Street loco got himself shot for a truckload of water.
Fucked up, right?
I know. I shot him.
What do they say? Live by the sword?
There's gotta be a bullet out there with my name on it. And I'm ready for that shit.
But she's only seven. I need ten years.

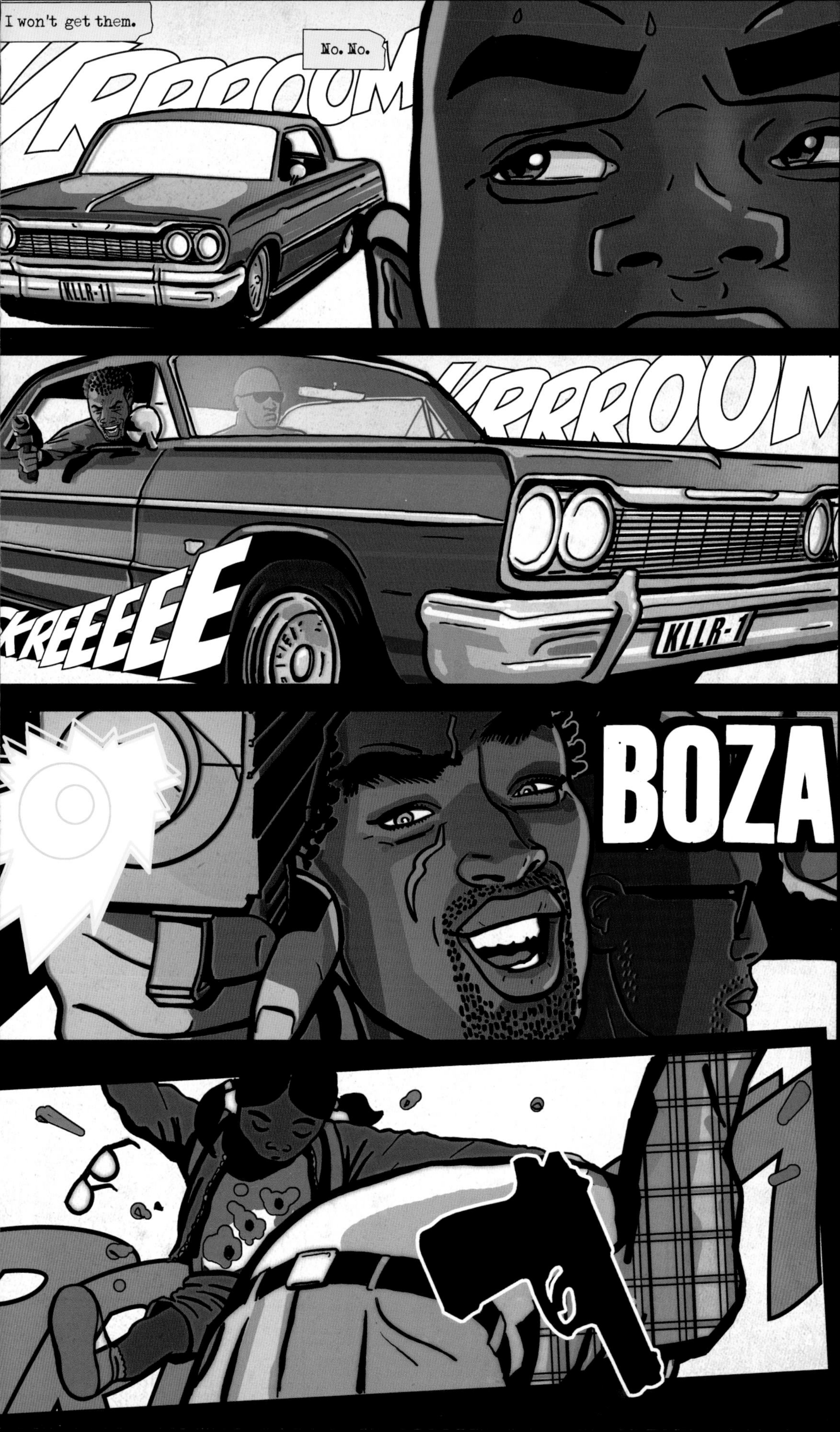

I won't get them.
No. No.
VRRROOOM
KLLR-1
VRRROOOM
SKREEEEE
KLLR-1
BOZA

Strange what you think about. I'm thinking, I know this ugly fool. I know that crooked smile.
That scar I gave him.
Got to remember to kill him.
TH-THUM
TH-THUMP
SKREEEEEE
TH-THUM
TH-THUMP
Rose.
WUP
WUP
WUP
POLIC
Rose.
POLIC
TH-THUMP

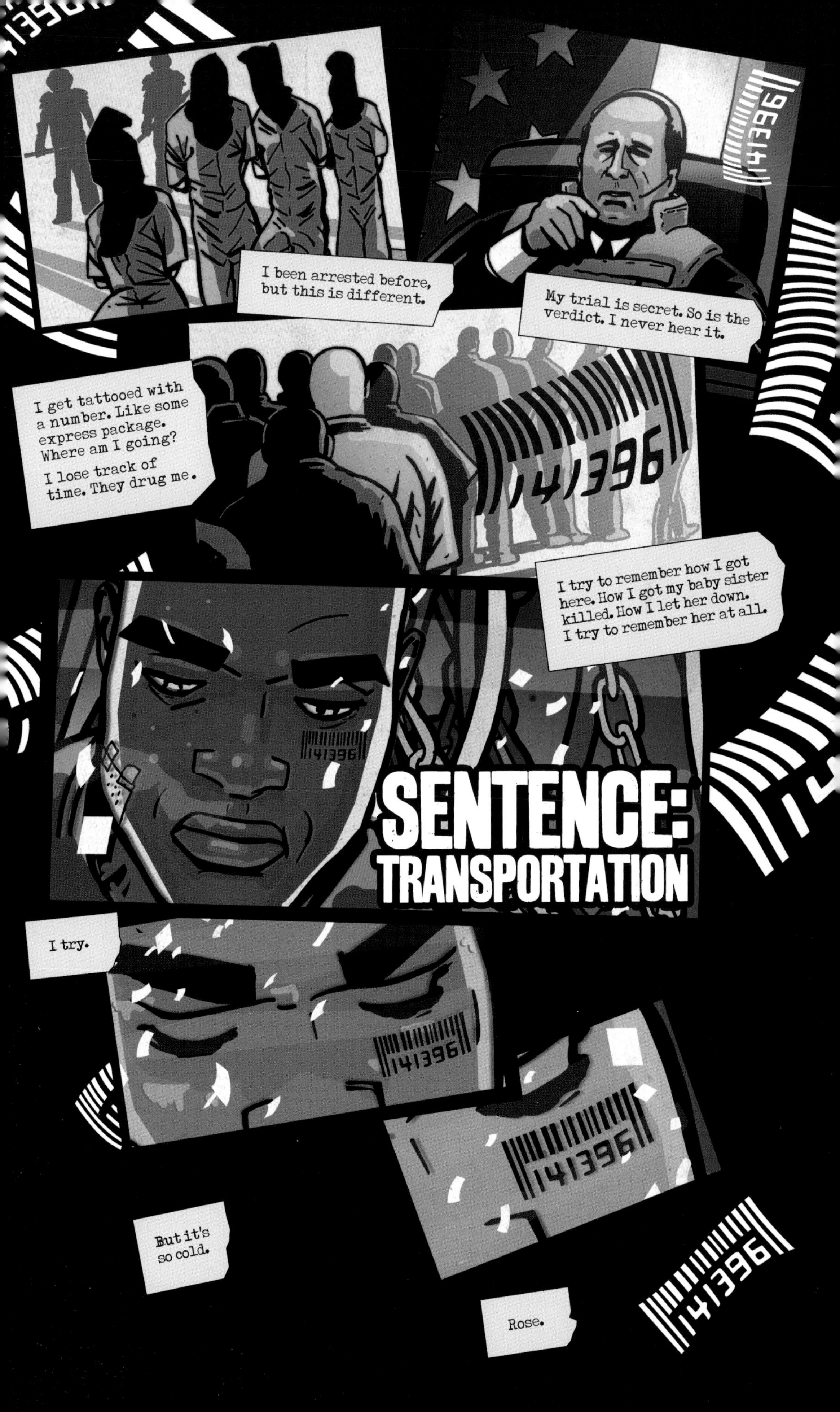
I been arrested before, but this is different.
My trial is secret. So is the verdict. I never hear it.
I get tattooed with a number. Like some express package. Where am I going?
I lose track of time. They drug me.
141396
I try to remember how I got here. How I got my baby sister killed. How I let her down. I try to remember her at all.
141396
SENTENCE: TRANSPORTATION
I try.
141396
141396
But it's so cold.
Rose.
141396

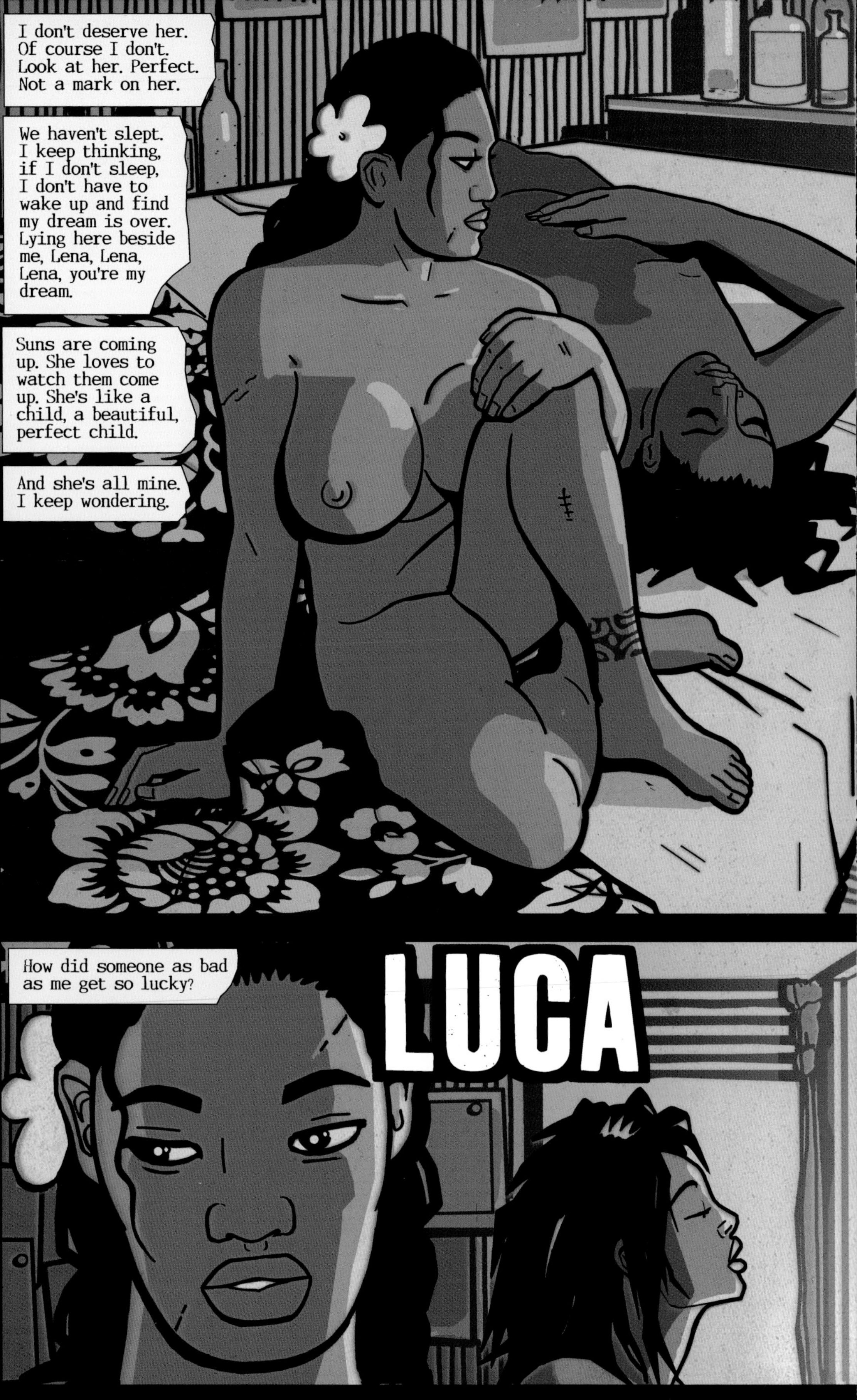
I don't deserve her. Of course I don't. Look at her. Perfect. Not a mark on her.
We haven't slept. I keep thinking, if I don't sleep, I don't have to wake up and find my dream is over. Lying here beside me, Lena, Lena, Lena, you're my dream.
Suns are coming up. She loves to watch them come up. She's like a child, a beautiful, perfect child.
And she's all mine. I keep wondering.
How did someone as bad as me get so lucky?
LUCA

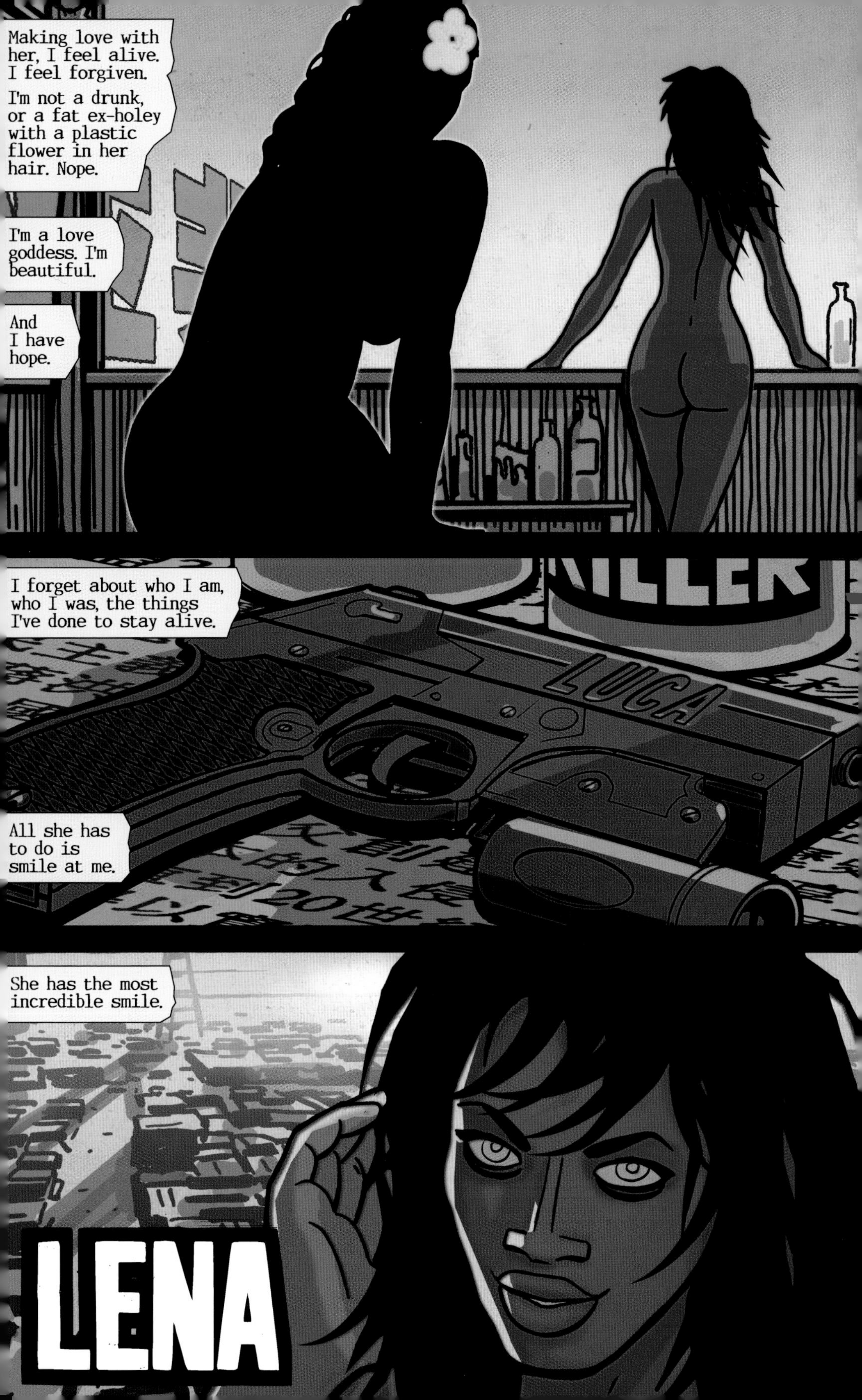
Making love with her, I feel alive. I feel forgiven.
I'm not a drunk, or a fat ex-holey with a plastic flower in her hair. Nope.
I'm a love goddess. I'm beautiful.
And I have hope.
KILLER
LUCA
I forget about who I am, who I was, the things I've done to stay alive.
All she has to do is smile at me.
She has the most incredible smile.
LENA

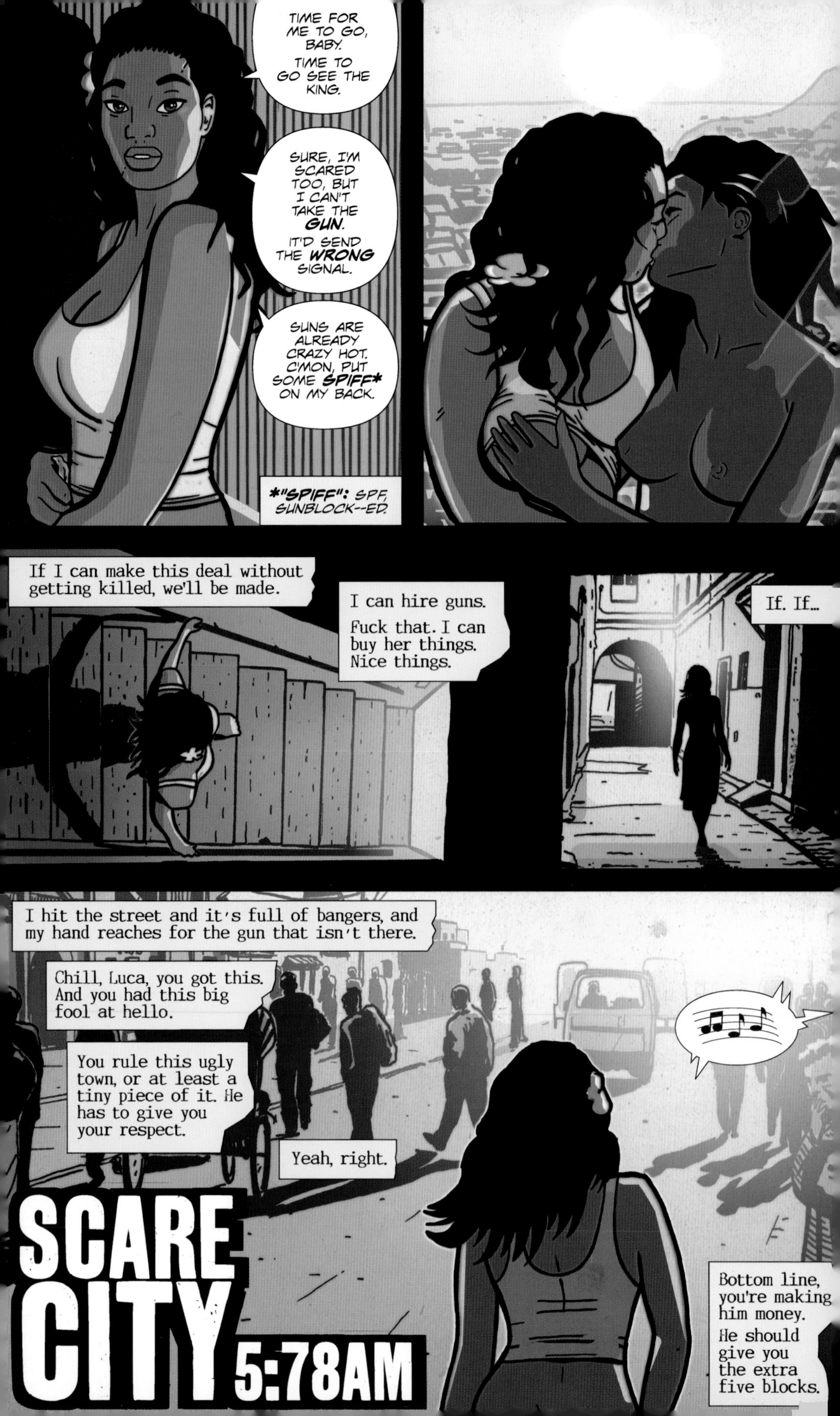
TIME FOR ME TO GO, BABY.
TIME TO GO SEE THE KING.
SURE, I'M SCARED TOO, BUT I CAN'T TAKE THE GUN.
IT'D SEND THE WRONG SIGNAL.
SUNS ARE ALREADY CRAZY HOT. C'MON, PUT SOME SPIFF* ON MY BACK.
*"SPIFF": SPF, SUNBLOCK--ED.
If I can make this deal without getting killed, we'll be made.
I can hire guns.
Fuck that. I can buy her things. Nice things.
If. If...
I hit the street and it's full of bangers, and my hand reaches for the gun that isn't there.
Chill, Luca, you got this. And you had this big fool at hello.
You rule this ugly town, or at least a tiny piece of it. He has to give you your respect.
Yeah, right.
SCARE CITY 5:78AM
Bottom line, you're making him money.
He should give you the extra five blocks.

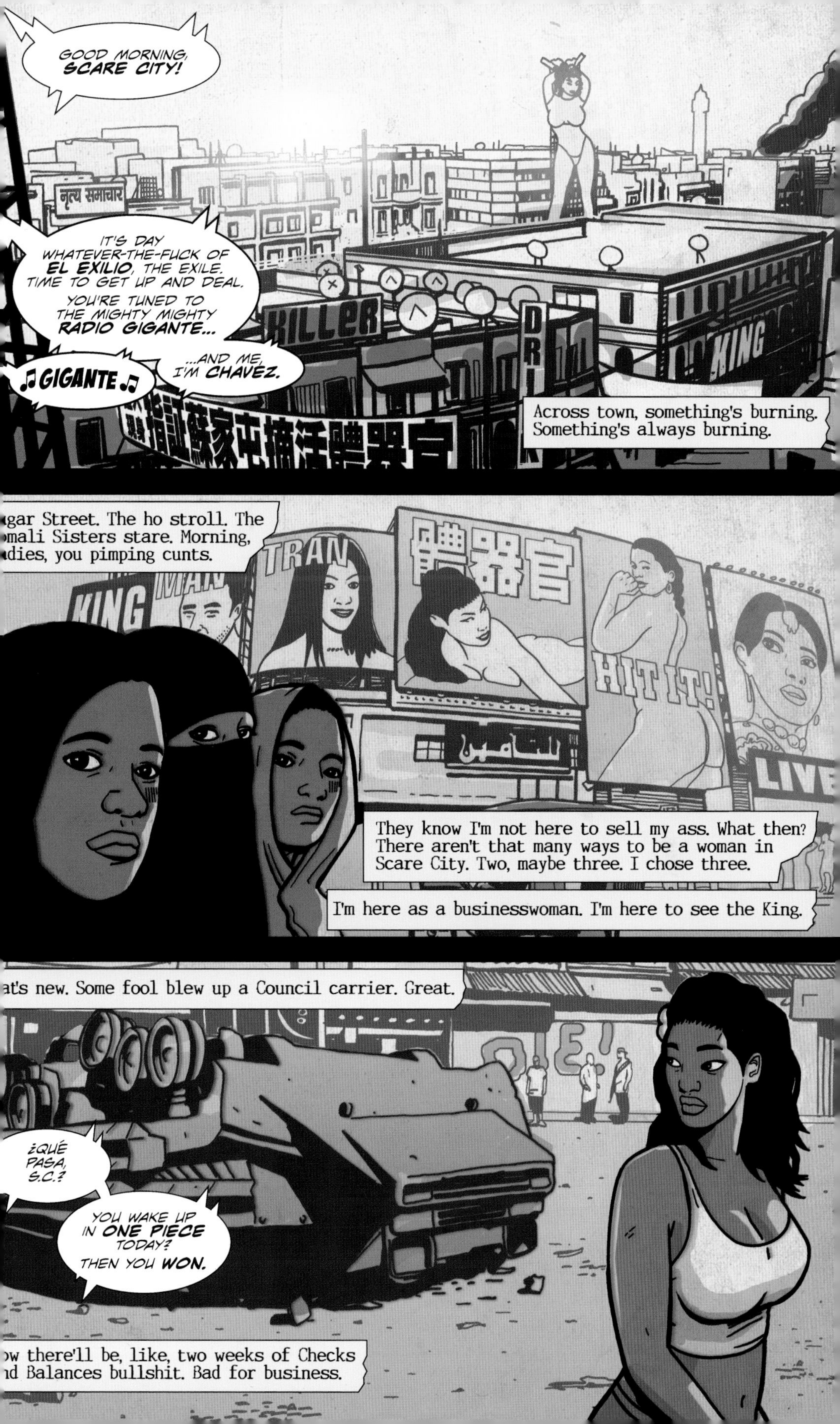
GOOD MORNING, SCARE CITY!
नृत्य समाचार
IT'S DAY WHATEVER-THE-FUCK OF EL EXILIO, THE EXILE. TIME TO GET UP AND DEAL. YOU'RE TUNED TO THE MIGHTY MIGHTY RADIO GIGANTE...
KILLER
KING
♫GIGANTE♫
...AND ME, I'M CHAVEZ.
Across town, something's burning. Something's always burning.
gar Street. The ho stroll. The
mali Sisters stare. Morning,
dies, you pimping cunts.
KING
TRAN
體器官
HIT IT!
LIVE
They know I'm not here to sell my ass. What then? There aren't that many ways to be a woman in Scare City. Two, maybe three. I chose three.
I'm here as a businesswoman. I'm here to see the King.
at's new. Some fool blew up a Council carrier. Great.
¿QUÉ PASA, S.C.?
YOU WAKE UP IN ONE PIECE TODAY? THEN YOU WON.
w there'll be, like, two weeks of Checks
d Balances bullshit. Bad for business.

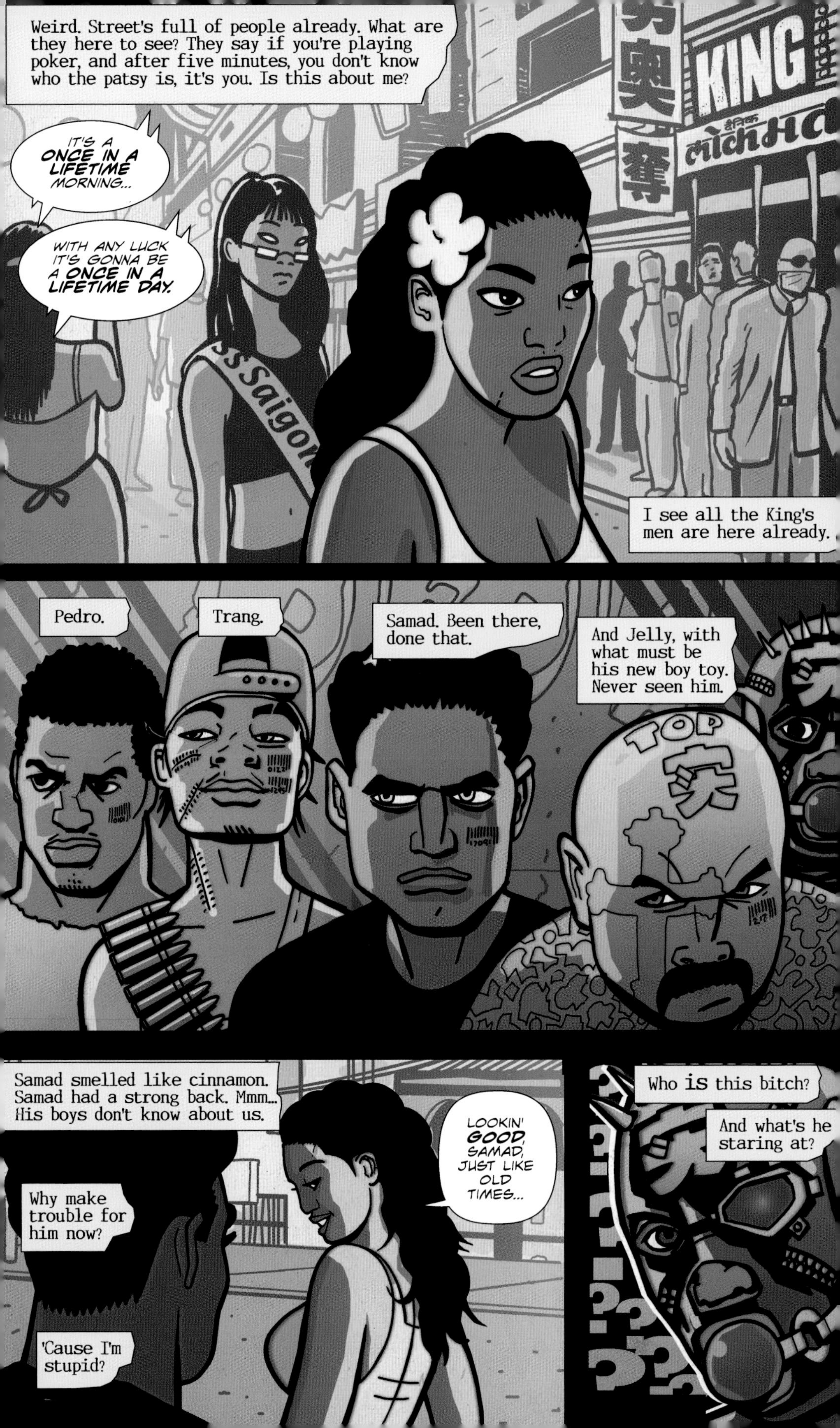

Weird. Street's full of people already. What are they here to see? They say if you're playing poker, and after five minutes, you don't know who the patsy is, it's you. Is this about me?
KING
IT'S A ONCE IN A LIFETIME MORNING...
WITH ANY LUCK IT'S GONNA BE A ONCE IN A LIFETIME DAY.
I see all the King's men are here already.
Pedro.
Trang.
Samad. Been there, done that.
And Jelly, with what must be his new boy toy. Never seen him.
TOP
Samad smelled like cinnamon. Samad had a strong back. Mmm... His boys don't know about us.
LOOKIN' GOOD, SAMAD, JUST LIKE OLD TIMES...
Why make trouble for him now?
'Cause I'm stupid?
Who is this bitch?
And what's he staring at?

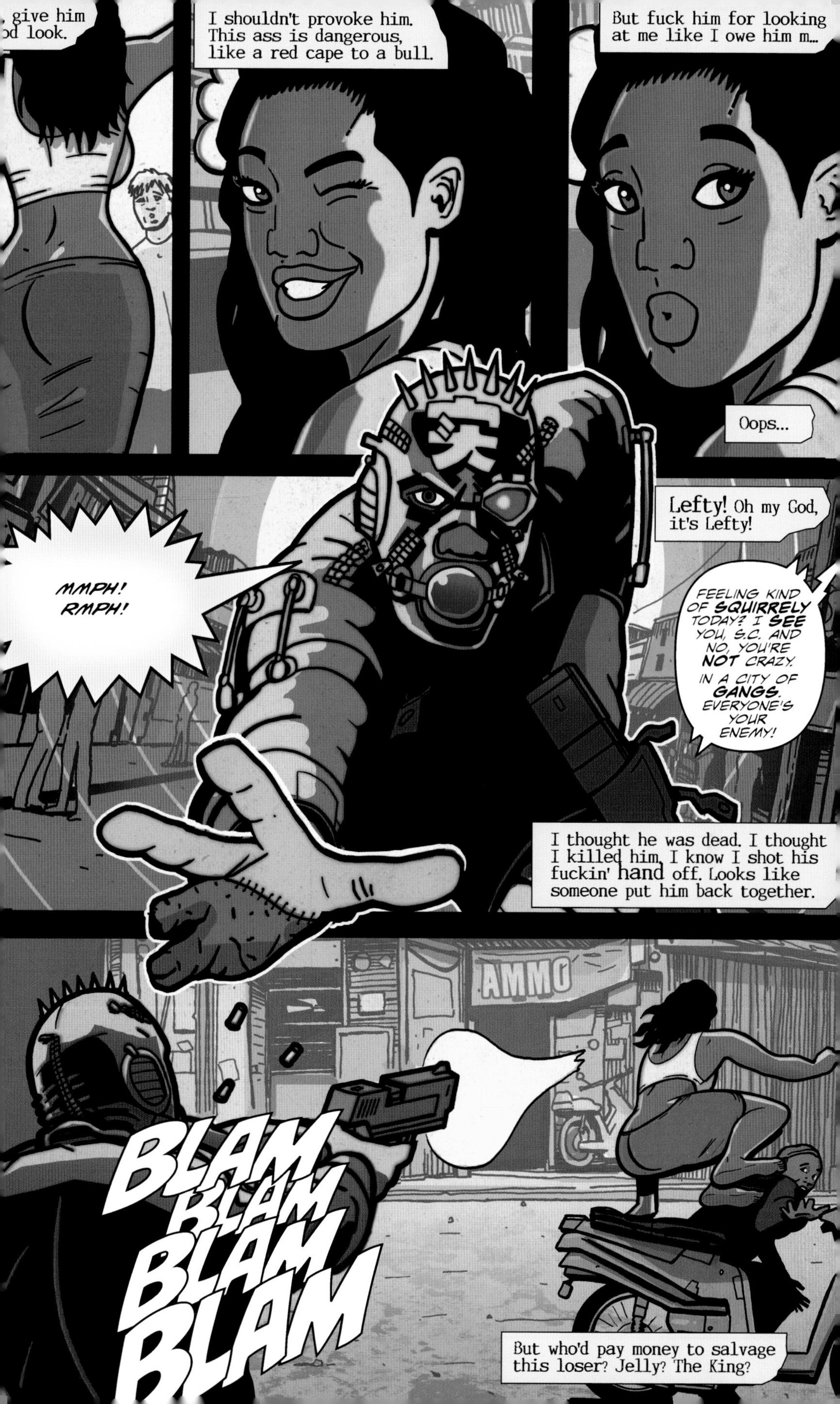

give him
od look.
I shouldn't provoke him. This ass is dangerous, like a red cape to a bull.
But fuck him for looking at me like I owe him m...
Oops...
Lefty! Oh my God, it's Lefty!
MMPH! RMPH!
FEELING KIND OF SQUIRRELY TODAY? I SEE YOU, S.C. AND NO, YOU'RE NOT CRAZY. IN A CITY OF GANGS, EVERYONE'S YOUR ENEMY!
I thought he was dead. I thought I killed him. I know I shot his fuckin' hand off. Looks like someone put him back together.
AMMO
BLAM BLAM BLAM BLAM
But who'd pay money to salvage this loser? Jelly? The King?

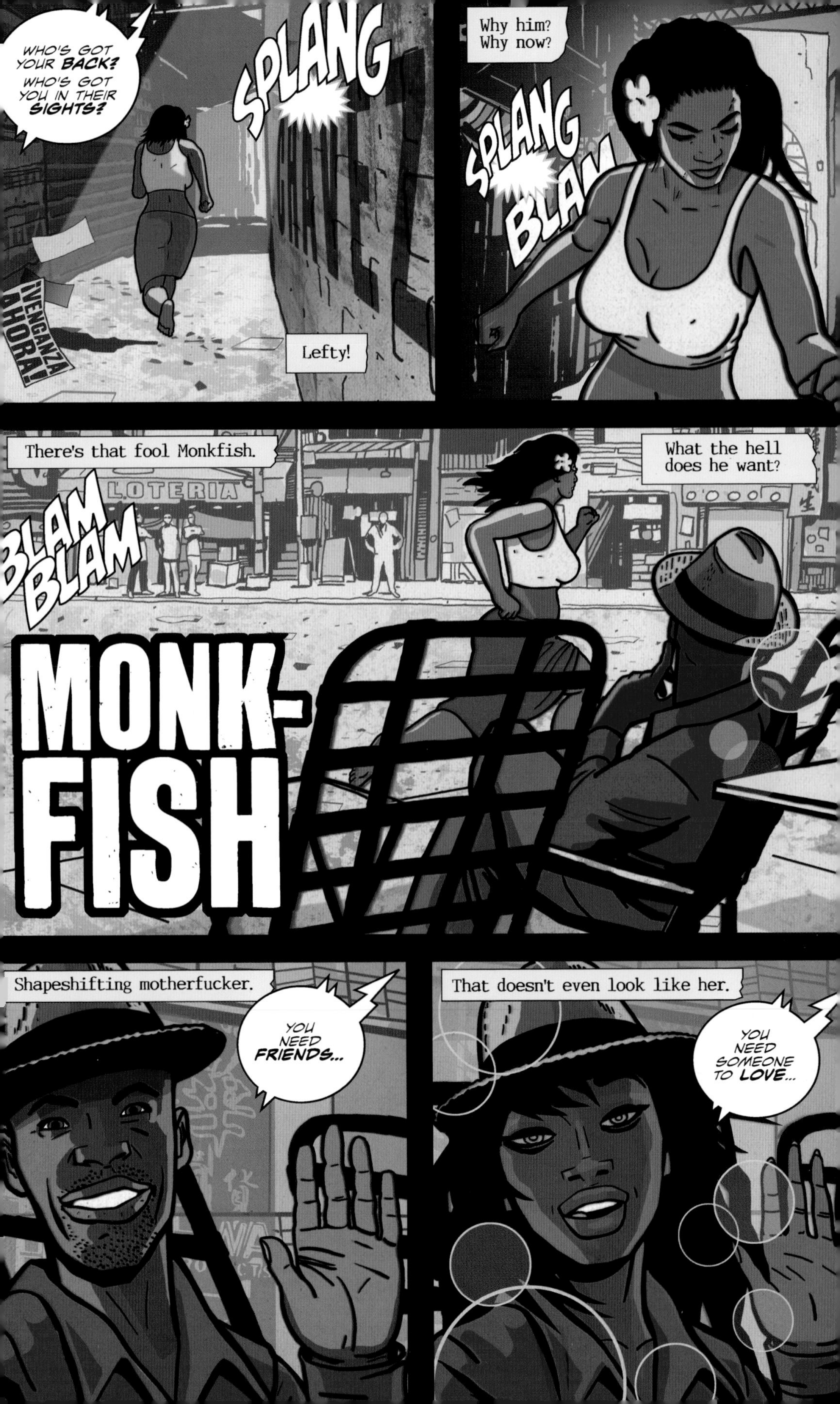
WHO'S GOT YOUR BACK? WHO'S GOT YOU IN THEIR SIGHTS?
SPLANG
¡VENGANZA AHORA!
Lefty!
Why him? Why now?
SPLANG
BLAM
There's that fool Monkfish.
LOTERIA
BLAM BLAM
What the hell does he want?
MONK-FISH
Shapeshifting motherfucker.
YOU NEED FRIENDS...
That doesn't even look like her.
YOU NEED SOMEONE TO LOVE...

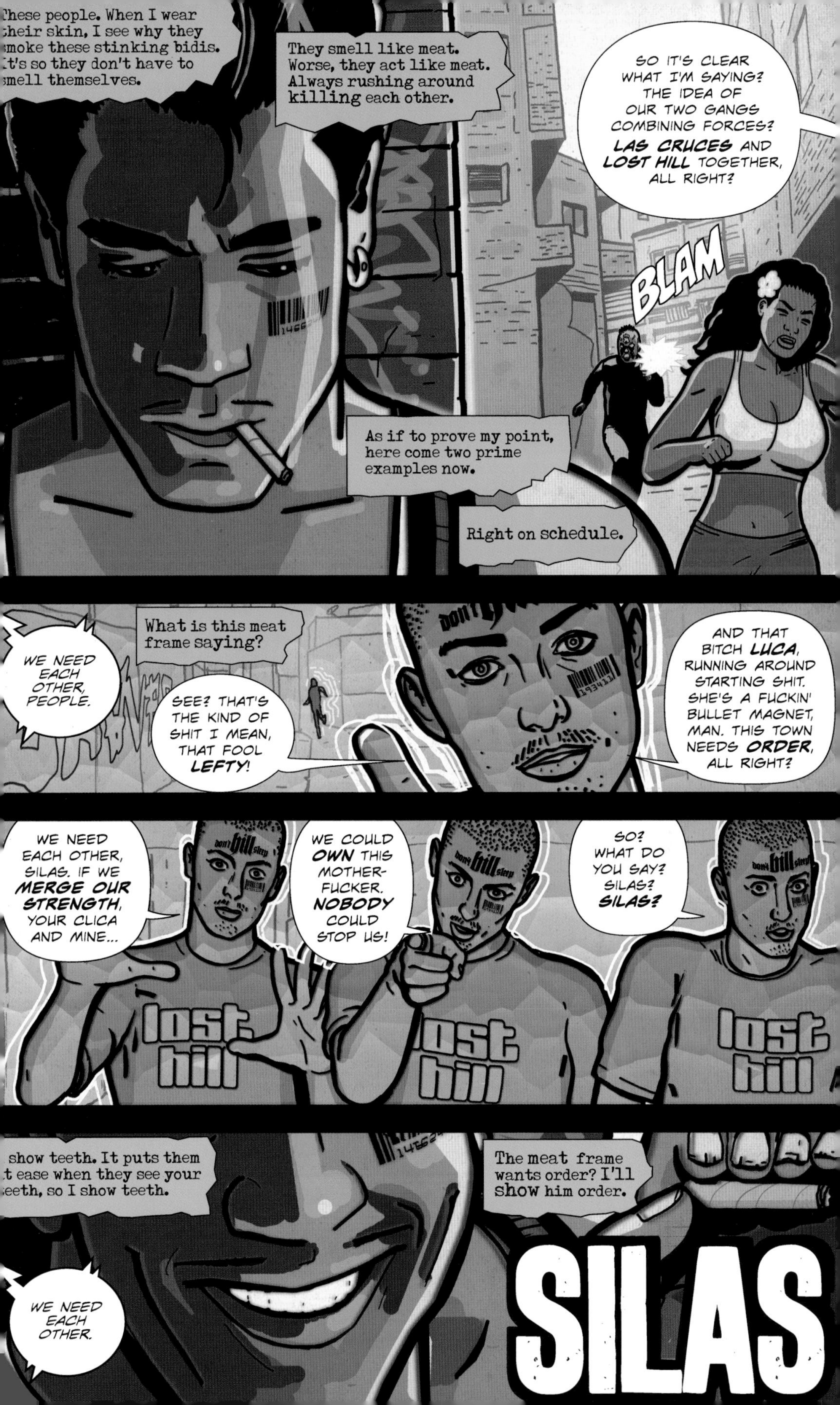
These people. When I wear their skin, I see why they smoke these stinking bidis. It's so they don't have to smell themselves.
They smell like meat. Worse, they act like meat. Always rushing around killing each other.
SO IT'S CLEAR WHAT I'M SAYING? THE IDEA OF OUR TWO GANGS COMBINING FORCES? LAS CRUCES AND LOST HILL TOGETHER, ALL RIGHT?
BLAM
As if to prove my point, here come two prime examples now.
Right on schedule.
WE NEED EACH OTHER, PEOPLE.
What is this meat frame saying?
SEE? THAT'S THE KIND OF SHIT I MEAN, THAT FOOL LEFTY!
AND THAT BITCH LUCA, RUNNING AROUND STARTING SHIT. SHE'S A FUCKIN' BULLET MAGNET, MAN. THIS TOWN NEEDS ORDER, ALL RIGHT?
WE NEED EACH OTHER, SILAS. IF WE MERGE OUR STRENGTH, YOUR CLICA AND MINE...
WE COULD OWN THIS MOTHER-FUCKER. NOBODY COULD STOP US!
SO? WHAT DO YOU SAY? SILAS? SILAS?
lost hill
lost hill
lost hill
show teeth. It puts them t ease when they see your eeth, so I show teeth.
The meat frame wants order? I'll show him order.
WE NEED EACH OTHER.
SILAS

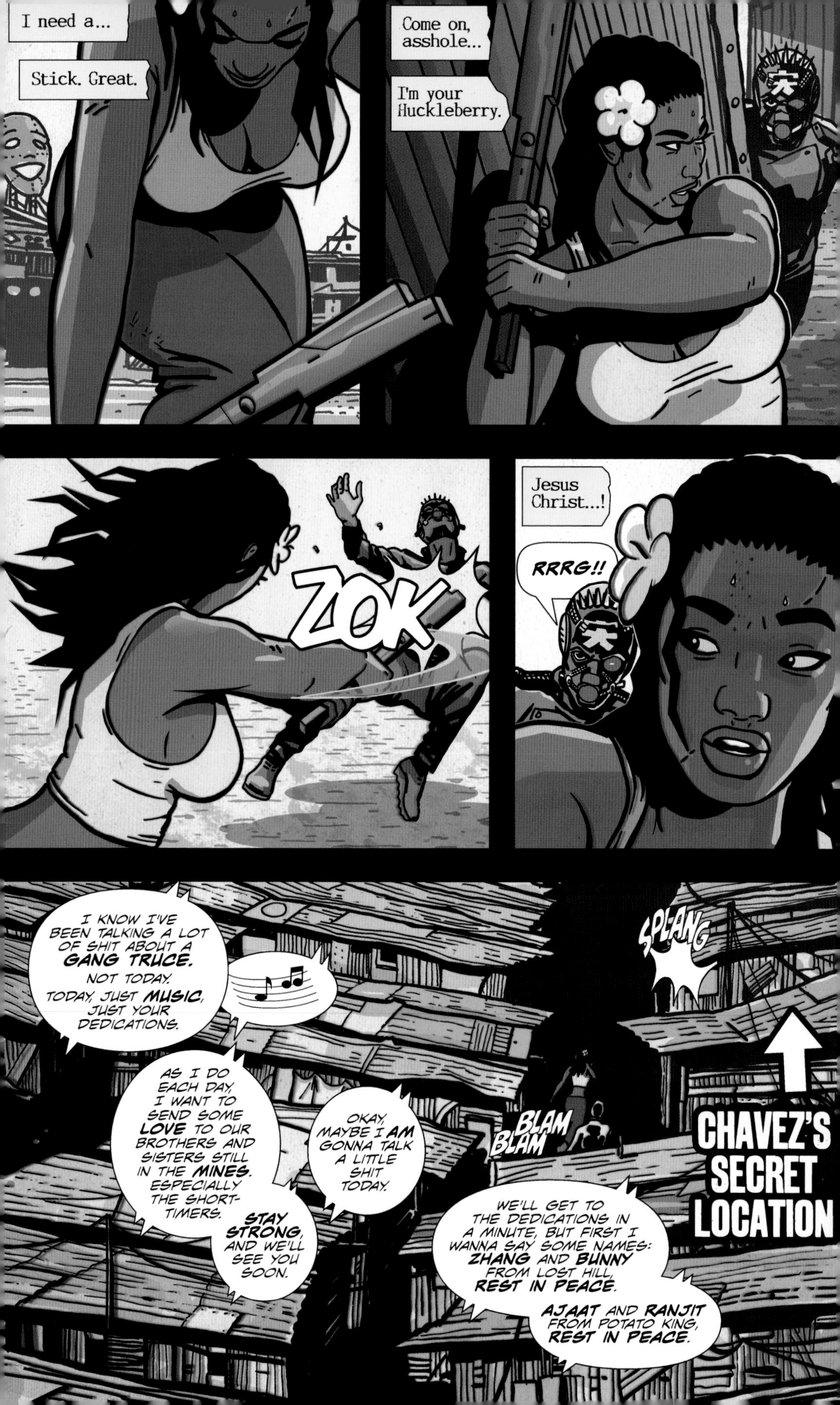

I need a...
Stick. Great.
Come on, asshole...
I'm your Huckleberry.
ZOK
Jesus Christ...!
RRRG!!
I KNOW I'VE BEEN TALKING A LOT OF SHIT ABOUT A GANG TRUCE. NOT TODAY. TODAY, JUST MUSIC, JUST YOUR DEDICATIONS.
AS I DO EACH DAY, I WANT TO SEND SOME LOVE TO OUR BROTHERS AND SISTERS STILL IN THE MINES. ESPECIALLY THE SHORT-TIMERS.
STAY STRONG, AND WE'LL SEE YOU SOON.
OKAY, MAYBE I AM GONNA TALK A LITTLE SHIT TODAY.
SPLANG
BLAM BLAM
WE'LL GET TO THE DEDICATIONS IN A MINUTE, BUT FIRST I WANNA SAY SOME NAMES: ZHANG AND BUNNY FROM LOST HILL, REST IN PEACE.
AJAAT AND RANJIT FROM POTATO KING, REST IN PEACE.
CHAVEZ'S SECRET LOCATION

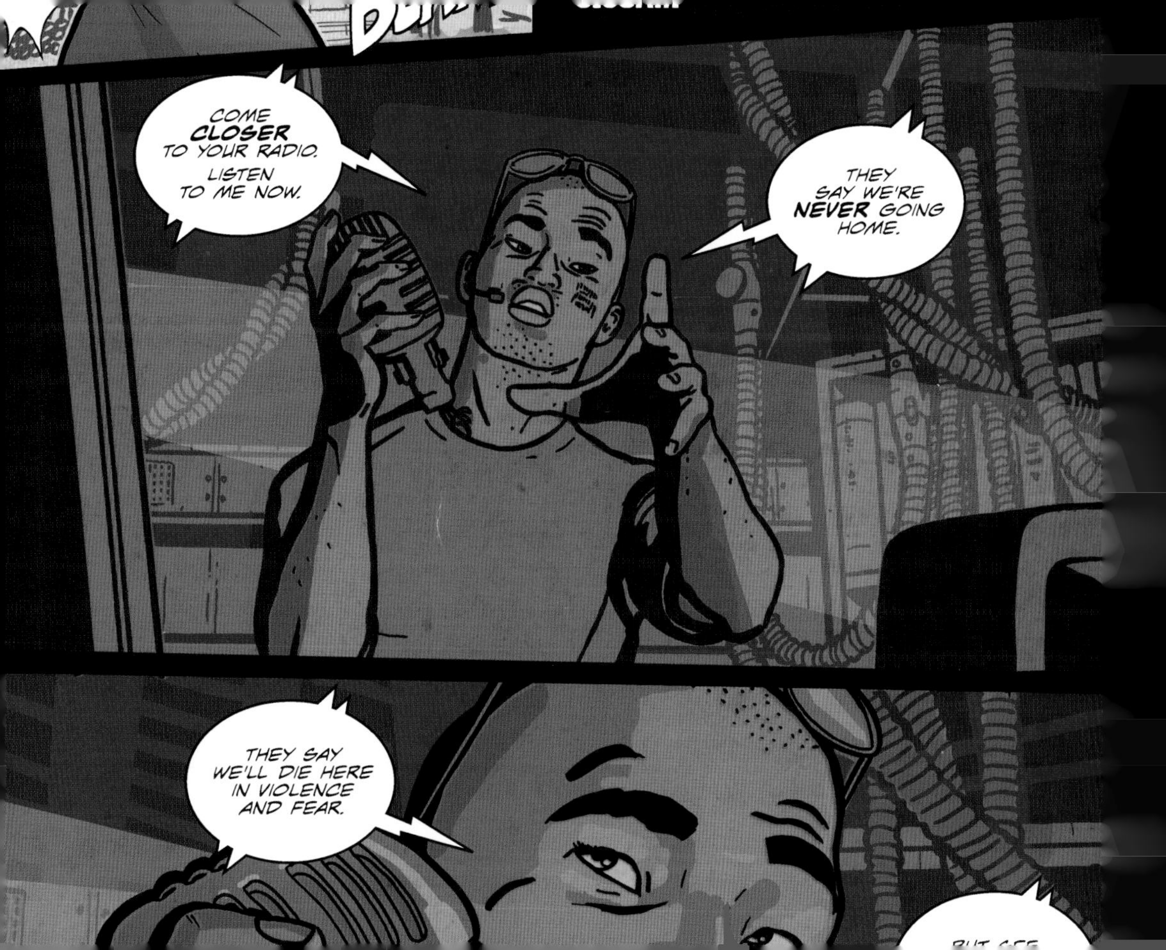
COME CLOSER TO YOUR RADIO. LISTEN TO ME NOW.
THEY SAY WE'RE NEVER GOING HOME.
THEY SAY WE'LL DIE HERE IN VIOLENCE AND FEAR.

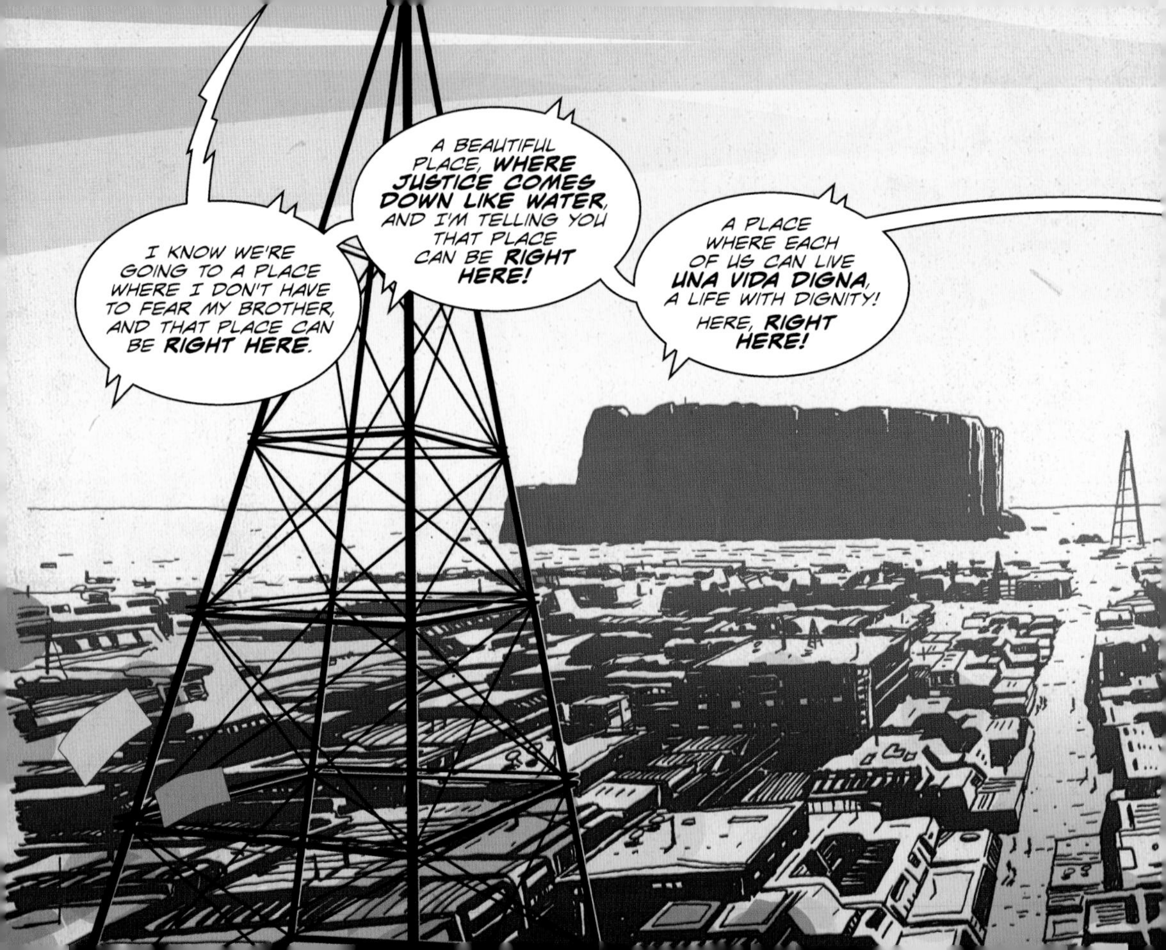
I KNOW WE'RE GOING TO A PLACE WHERE I DON'T HAVE TO FEAR MY BROTHER, AND THAT PLACE CAN BE **RIGHT HERE**.
A BEAUTIFUL PLACE, **WHERE JUSTICE COMES DOWN LIKE WATER**, AND I'M TELLING YOU THAT PLACE CAN BE **RIGHT HERE!**
A PLACE WHERE EACH OF US CAN LIVE **UNA VIDA DIGNA**, A LIFE WITH DIGNITY! HERE, **RIGHT HERE!**

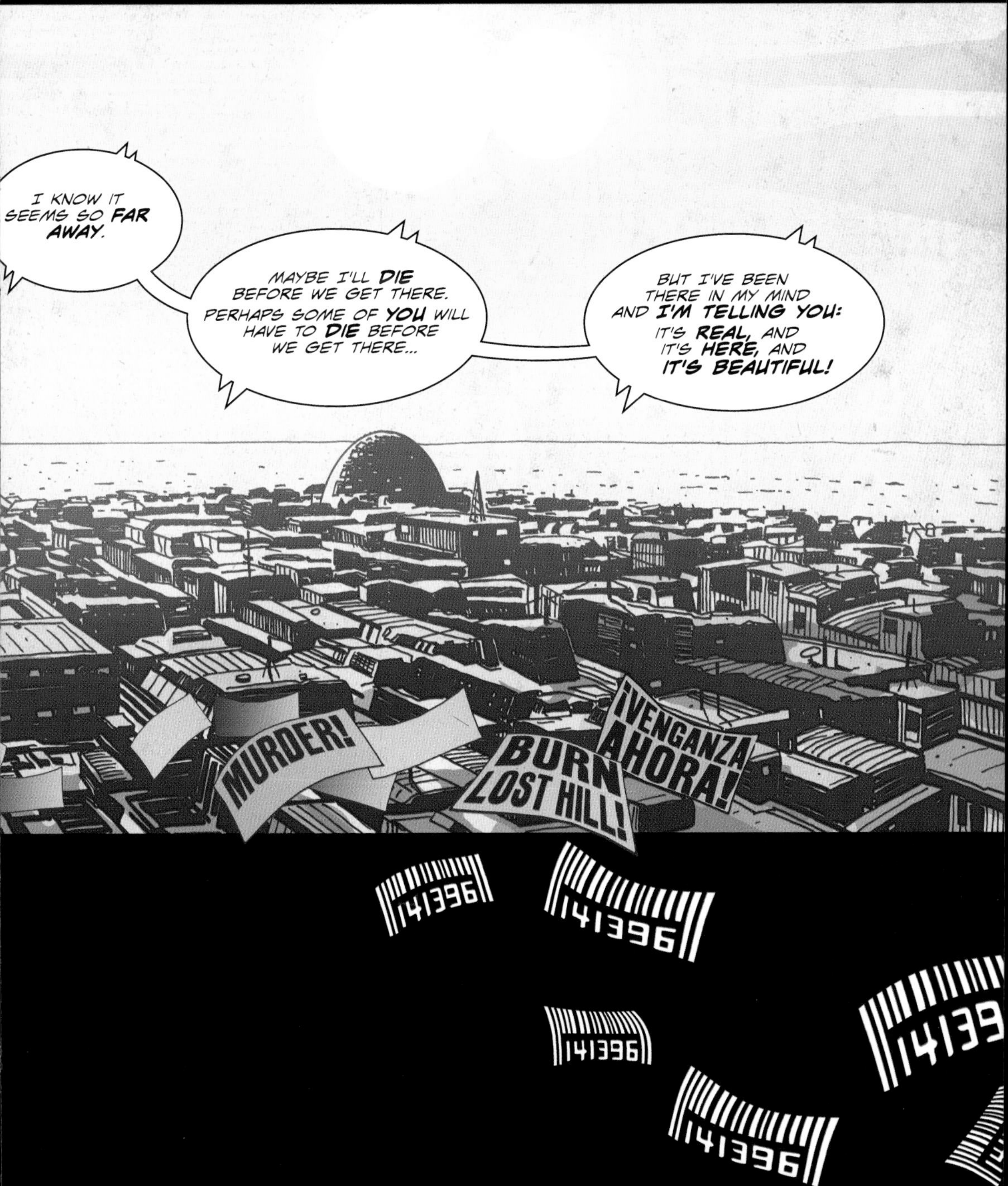
I KNOW IT SEEMS SO **FAR AWAY**.
MAYBE I'LL **DIE** BEFORE WE GET THERE. PERHAPS SOME OF **YOU** WILL HAVE TO **DIE** BEFORE WE GET THERE...
BUT I'VE BEEN THERE IN MY MIND AND **I'M TELLING YOU:** IT'S **REAL,** AND IT'S **HERE,** AND **IT'S BEAUTIFUL!**
MURDER!
BURN LOST HILL!
¡VENGANZA AHORA!
141396
141396
141396
141396
14139

ISAAC
CLINK
CLINK
RRRR
RRRR
It's snowing.
Is it snowing?
Why is it snowing?
Where am I?
How long have I
been like this?
RRRUMBLE

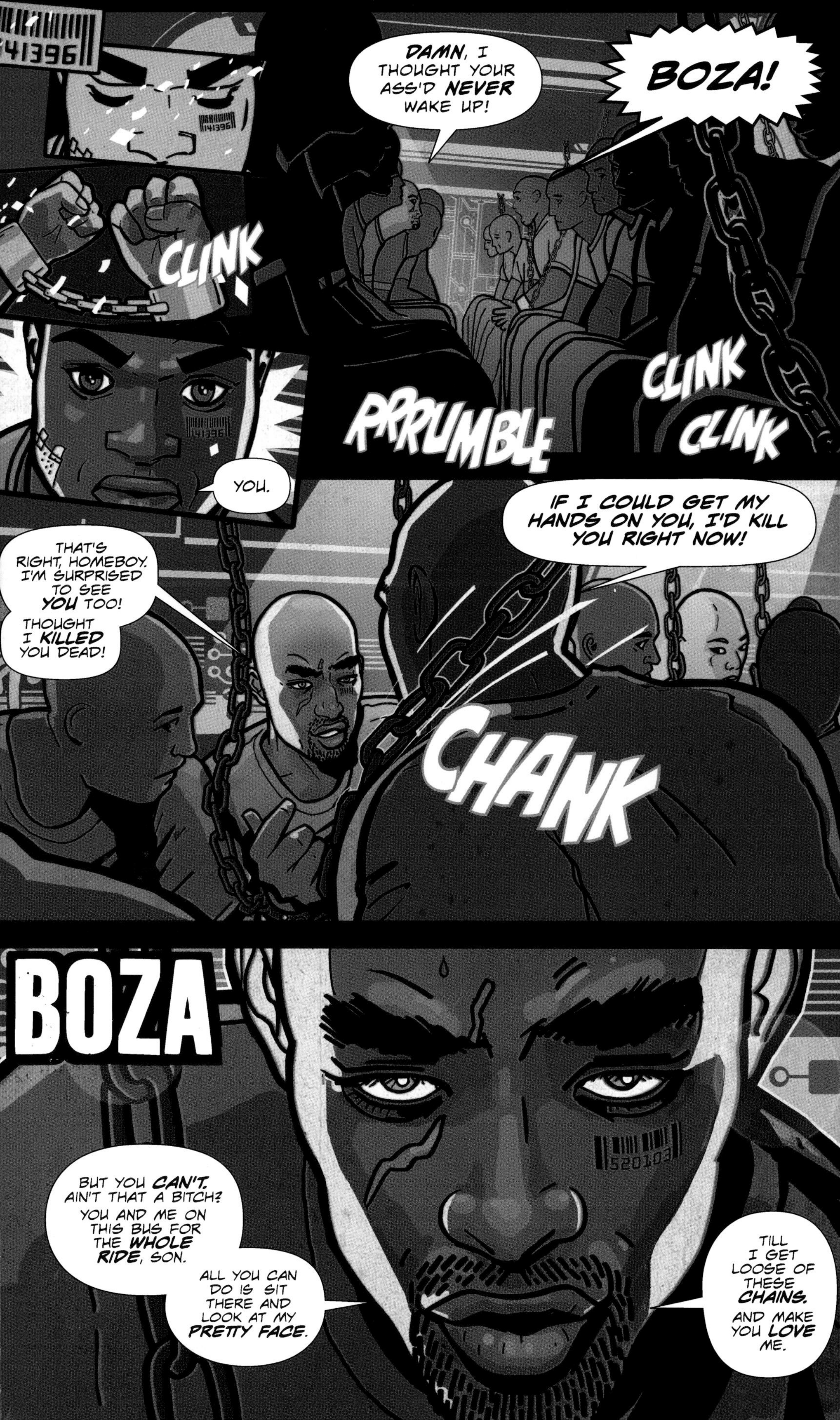

CLINK
DAMN, I THOUGHT YOUR ASS'D NEVER WAKE UP!
BOZA!
RRRUMBLE
CLINK
CLINK
YOU.
IF I COULD GET MY HANDS ON YOU, I'D KILL YOU RIGHT NOW!
THAT'S RIGHT, HOMEBOY. I'M SURPRISED TO SEE YOU TOO!
THOUGHT I KILLED YOU DEAD!
CHANK
BOZA
BUT YOU CAN'T. AIN'T THAT A BITCH?
YOU AND ME ON THIS BUS FOR THE WHOLE RIDE, SON.
ALL YOU CAN DO IS SIT THERE AND LOOK AT MY PRETTY FACE.
TILL I GET LOOSE OF THESE CHAINS.
AND MAKE YOU LOVE ME.

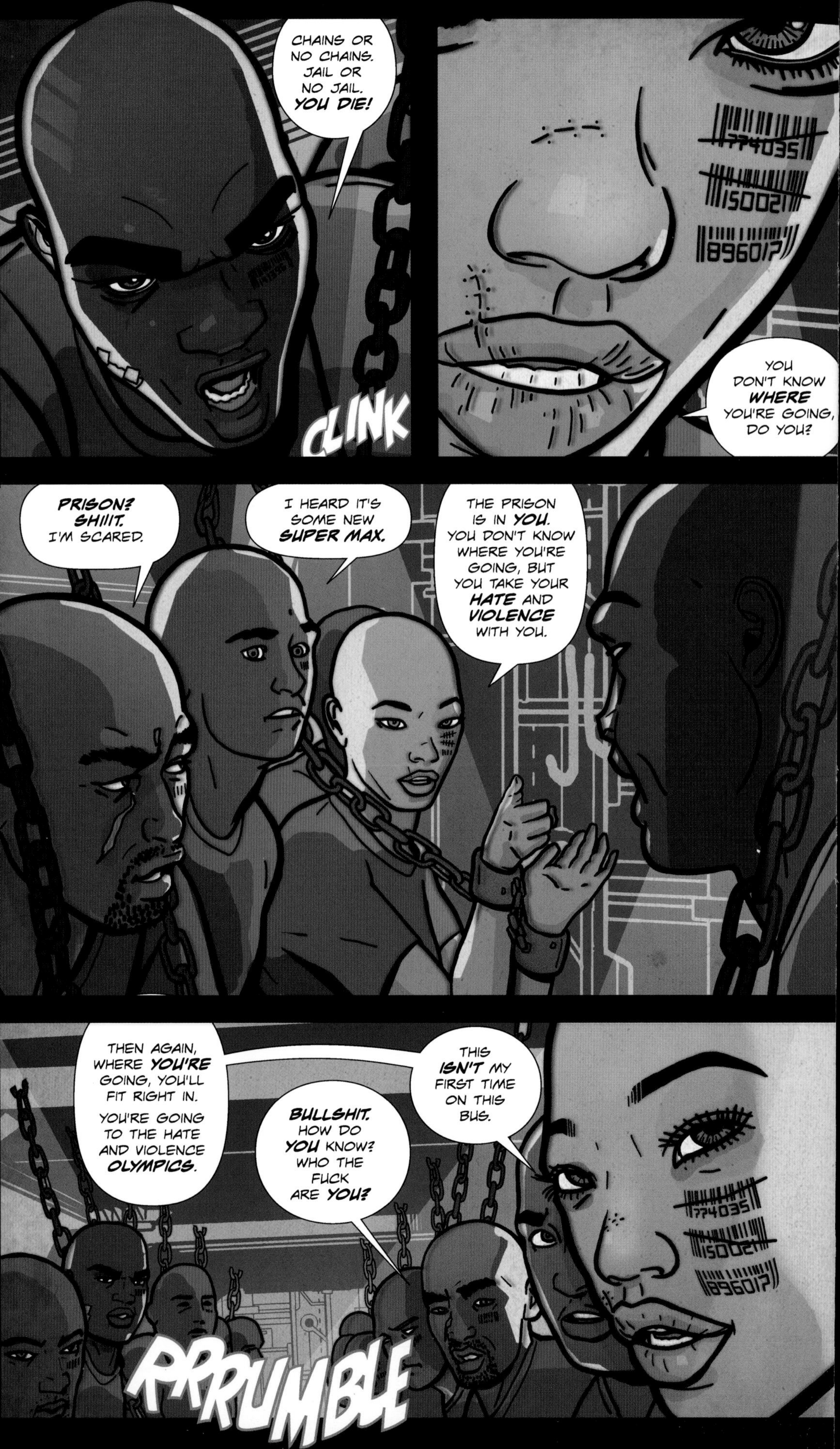
CHAINS OR NO CHAINS. JAIL OR NO JAIL. YOU DIE!
CLINK
YOU DON'T KNOW WHERE YOU'RE GOING, DO YOU?
PRISON? SHIIIT. I'M SCARED.
I HEARD IT'S SOME NEW SUPER MAX.
THE PRISON IS IN YOU. YOU DON'T KNOW WHERE YOU'RE GOING, BUT YOU TAKE YOUR HATE AND VIOLENCE WITH YOU.
THEN AGAIN, WHERE YOU'RE GOING, YOU'LL FIT RIGHT IN.
YOU'RE GOING TO THE HATE AND VIOLENCE OLYMPICS.
BULLSHIT. HOW DO YOU KNOW? WHO THE FUCK ARE YOU?
THIS ISN'T MY FIRST TIME ON THIS BUS.
RRRUMBLE

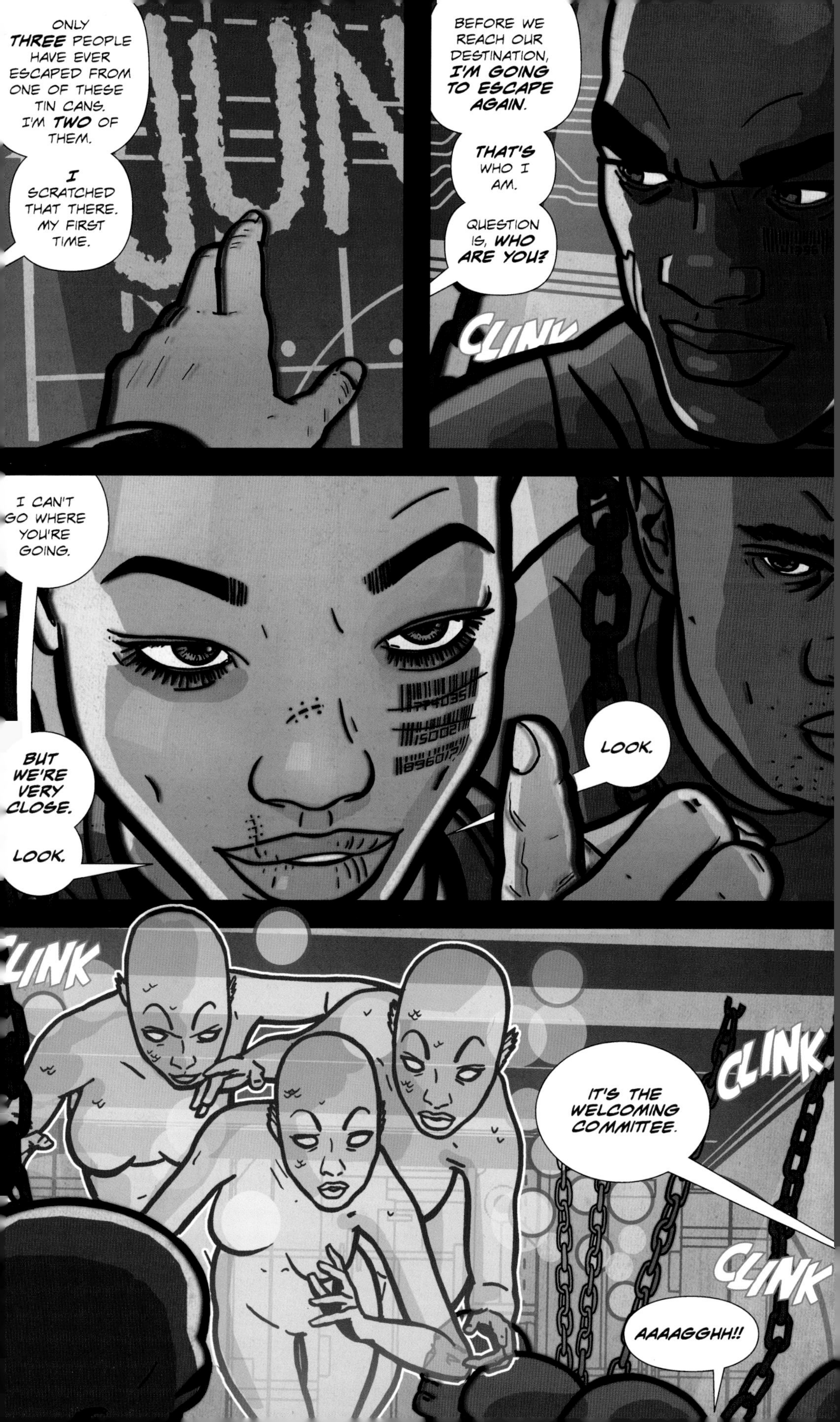
ONLY THREE PEOPLE HAVE EVER ESCAPED FROM ONE OF THESE TIN CANS. I'M TWO OF THEM.
I SCRATCHED THAT THERE. MY FIRST TIME.
BEFORE WE REACH OUR DESTINATION, I'M GOING TO ESCAPE AGAIN.
THAT'S WHO I AM.
QUESTION IS, WHO ARE YOU?
CLINK
I CAN'T GO WHERE YOU'RE GOING.
BUT WE'RE VERY CLOSE.
LOOK.
LOOK.
CLINK
CLINK
IT'S THE WELCOMING COMMITTEE.
CLINK
AAAAGGHH!!

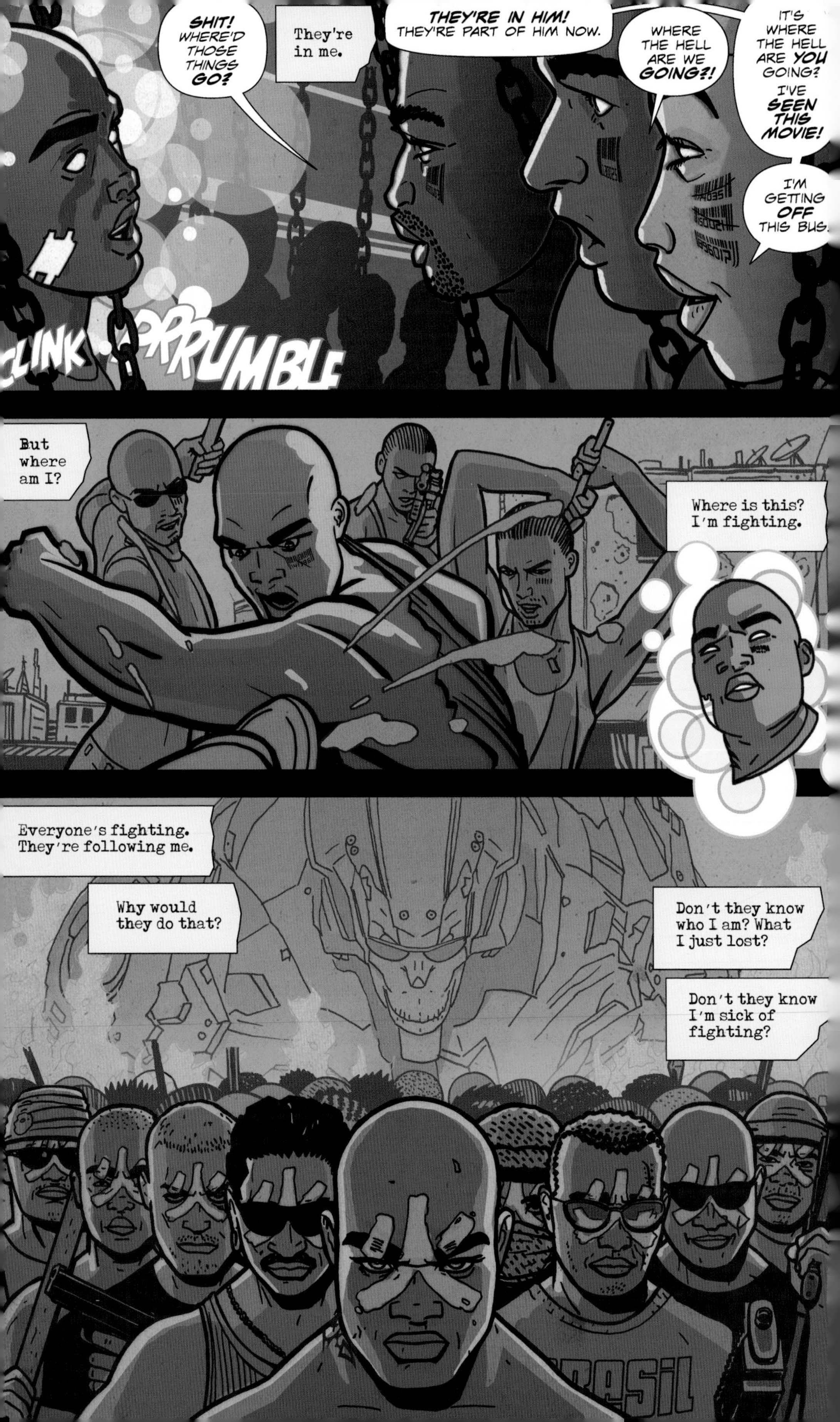
SHIT! WHERE'D THOSE THINGS GO?
They're in me.
THEY'RE IN HIM! THEY'RE PART OF HIM NOW.
WHERE THE HELL ARE WE GOING?!
IT'S WHERE THE HELL ARE YOU GOING? I'VE SEEN THIS MOVIE!
I'M GETTING OFF THIS BUS.
CLINK
RRRUMBLE
But where am I?
Where is this? I'm fighting.
Everyone's fighting. They're following me.
Why would they do that?
Don't they know who I am? What I just lost?
Don't they know I'm sick of fighting?

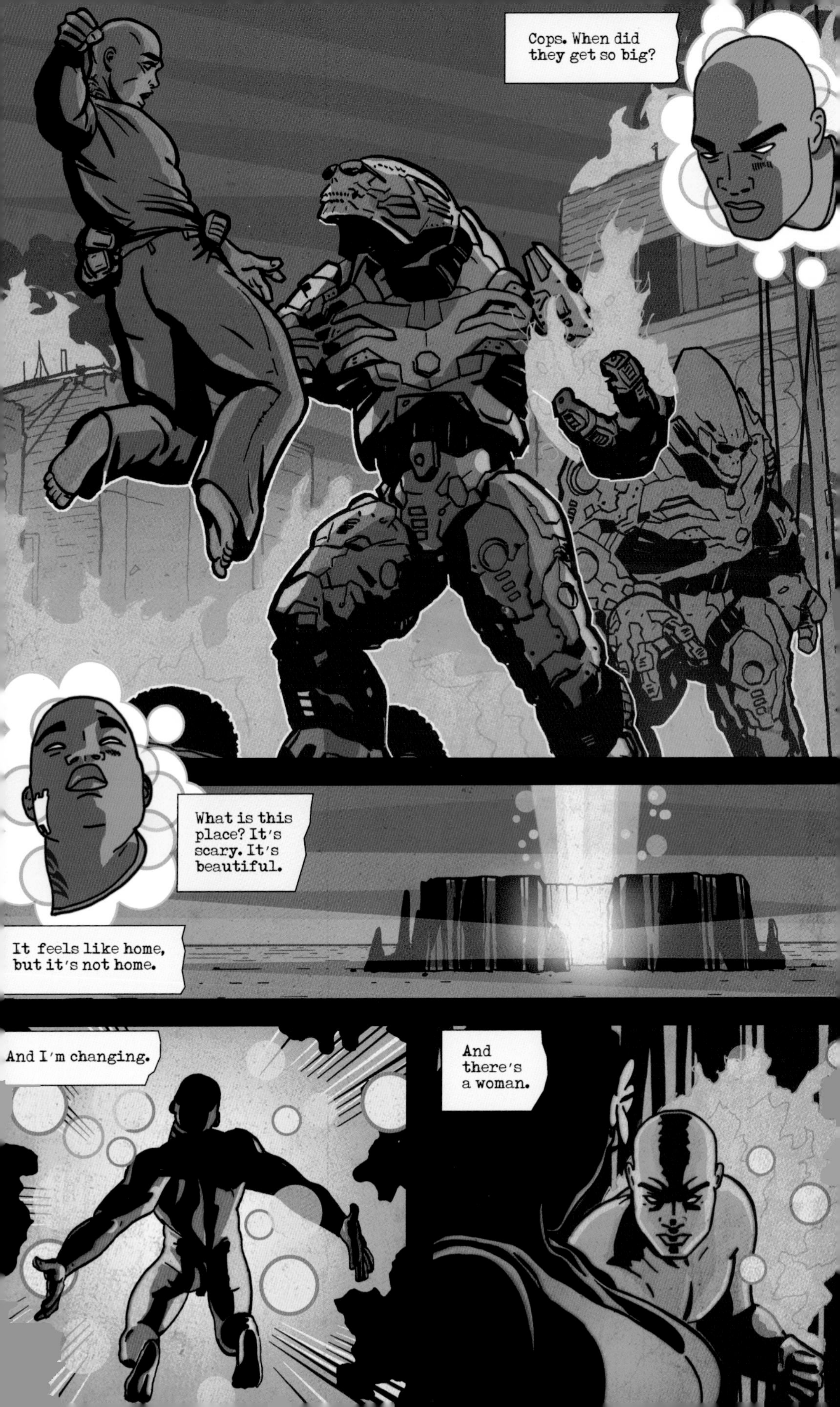
Cops. When did they get so big?
What is this place? It's scary. It's beautiful.
It feels like home, but it's not home.
And I'm changing.
And there's a woman.

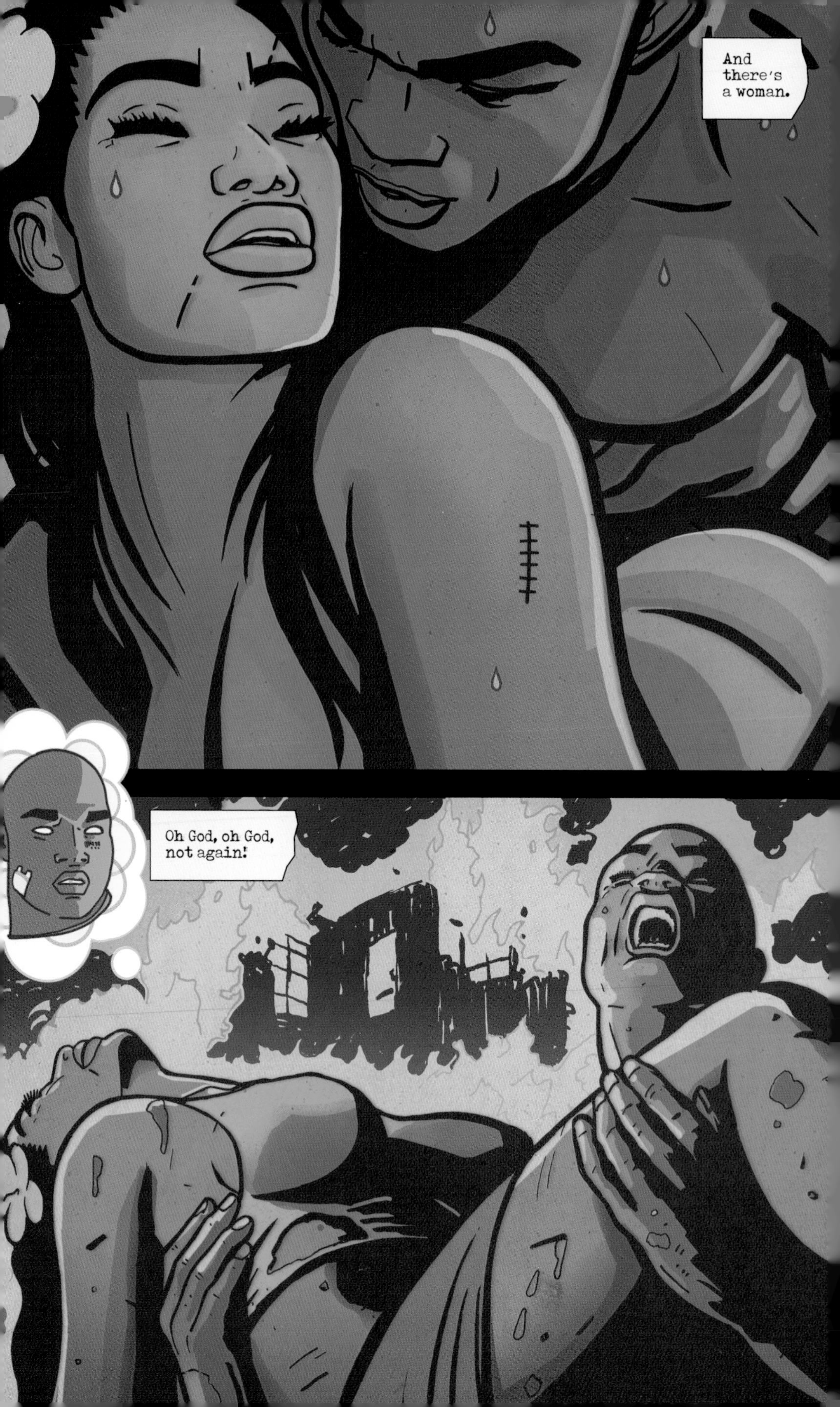
And there's a woman.
Oh God, oh God, not again!

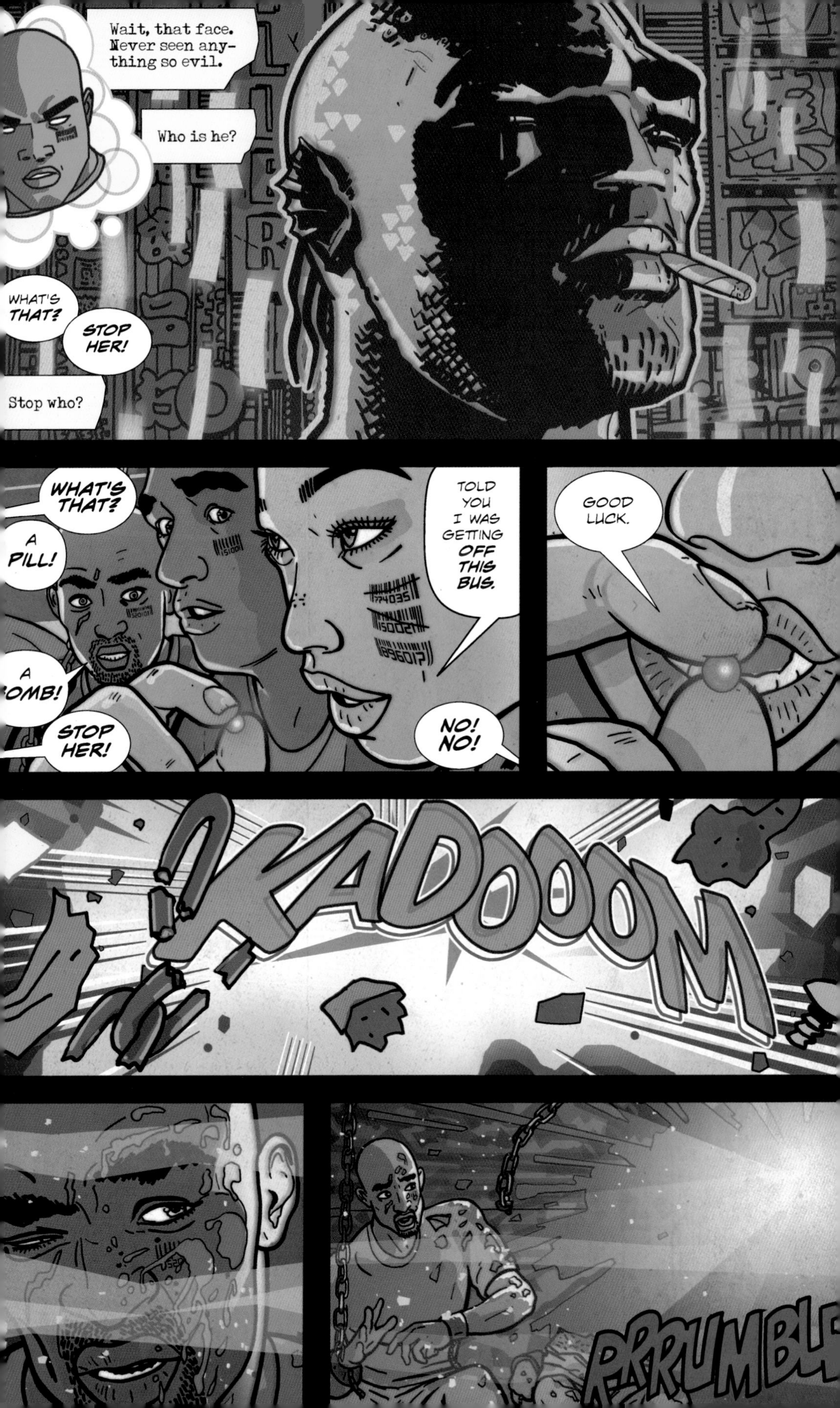

Wait, that face. Never seen any-thing so evil.
Who is he?
WHAT'S THAT?
STOP HER!
Stop who?
WHAT'S THAT?
A PILL!
A BOMB!
STOP HER!
TOLD YOU I WAS GETTING OFF THIS BUS.
NO! NO!
GOOD LUCK.
KADOOOM
PRRUMBLE

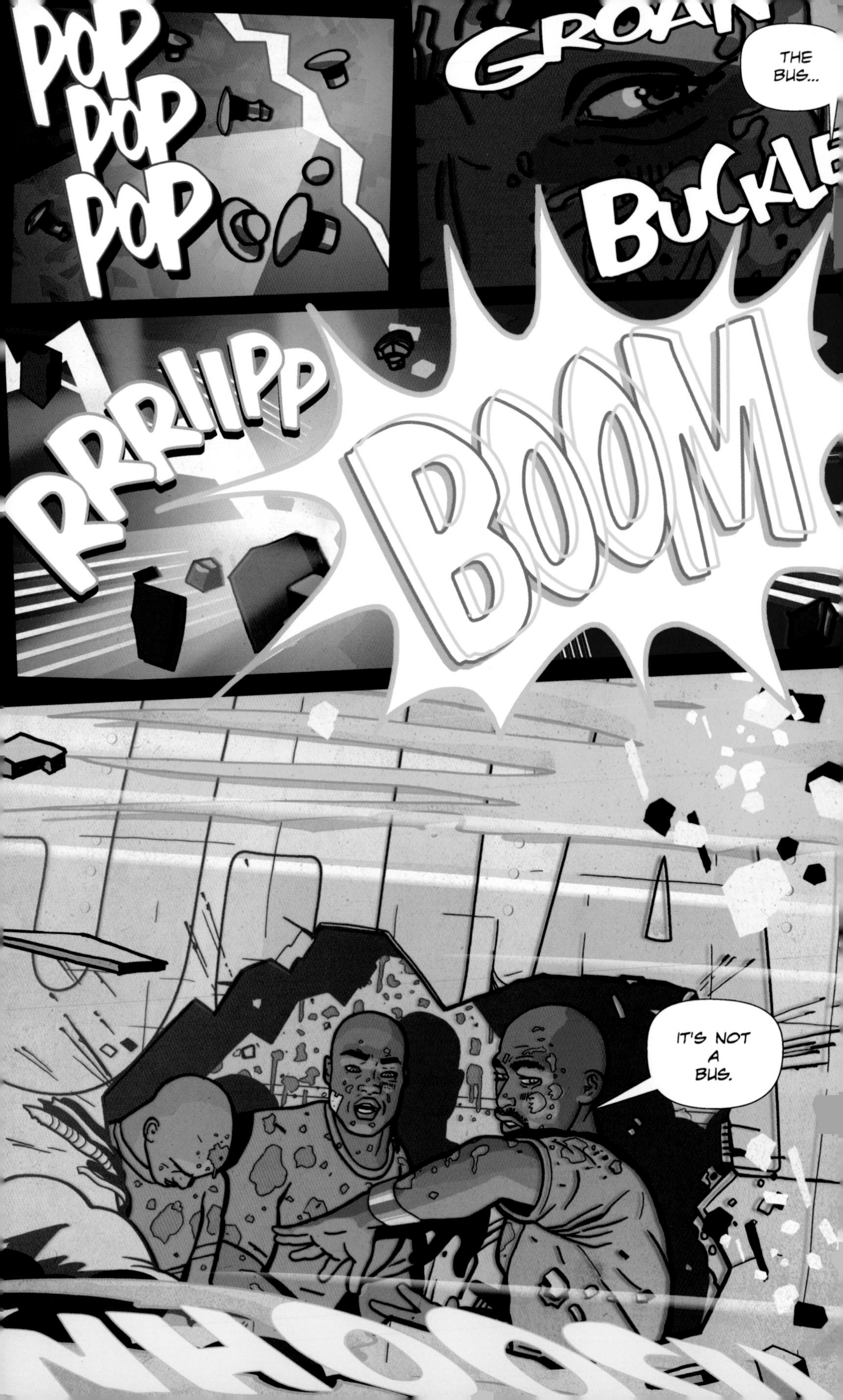
POP
POP
POP
GROAN
THE BUS...
BUCKLE
RRRIIPP
BOOOM
IT'S NOT A BUS.

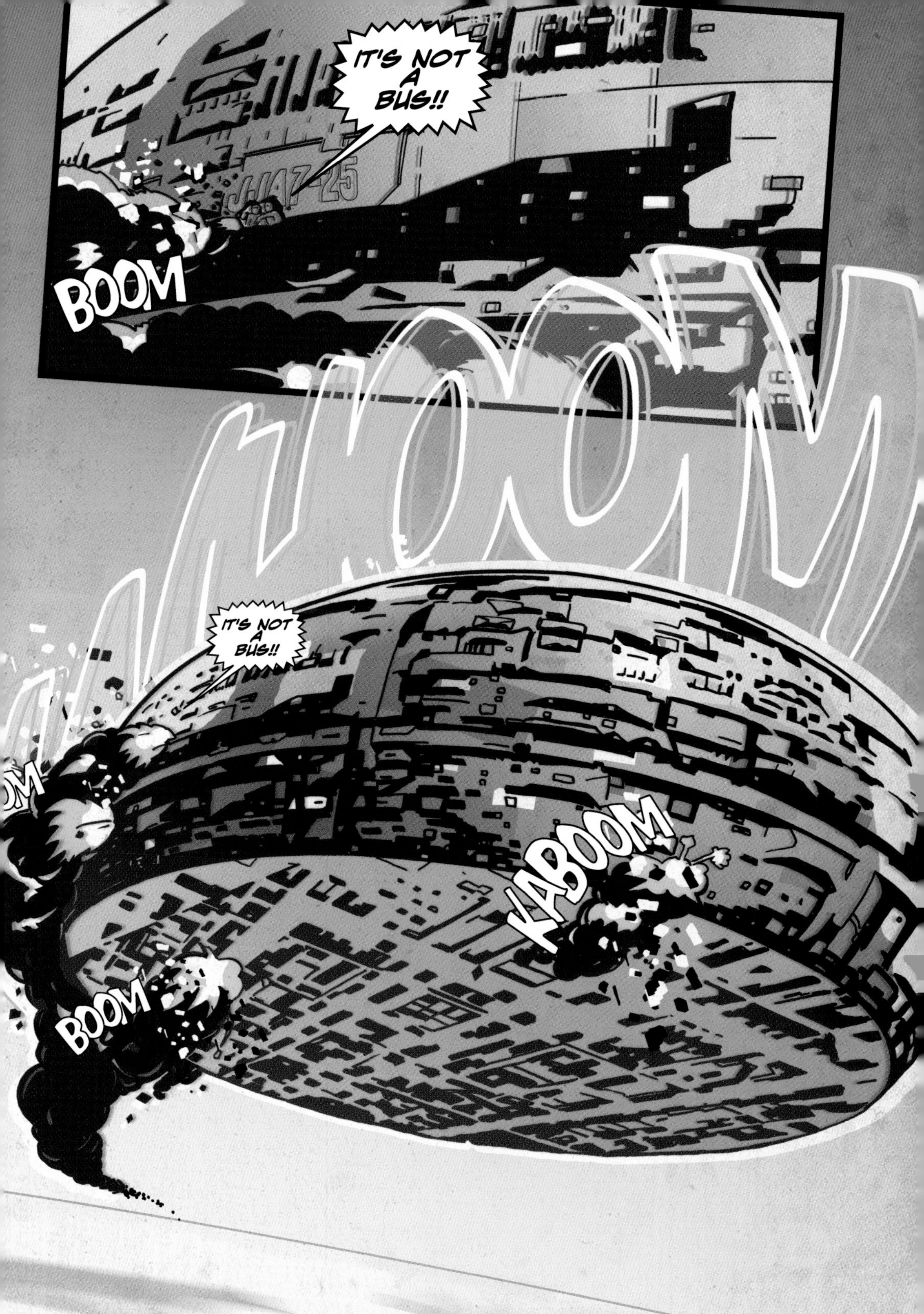
IT'S NOT A BUS!!
BOOM
IT'S NOT A BUS!!
KABOOM
BOOM

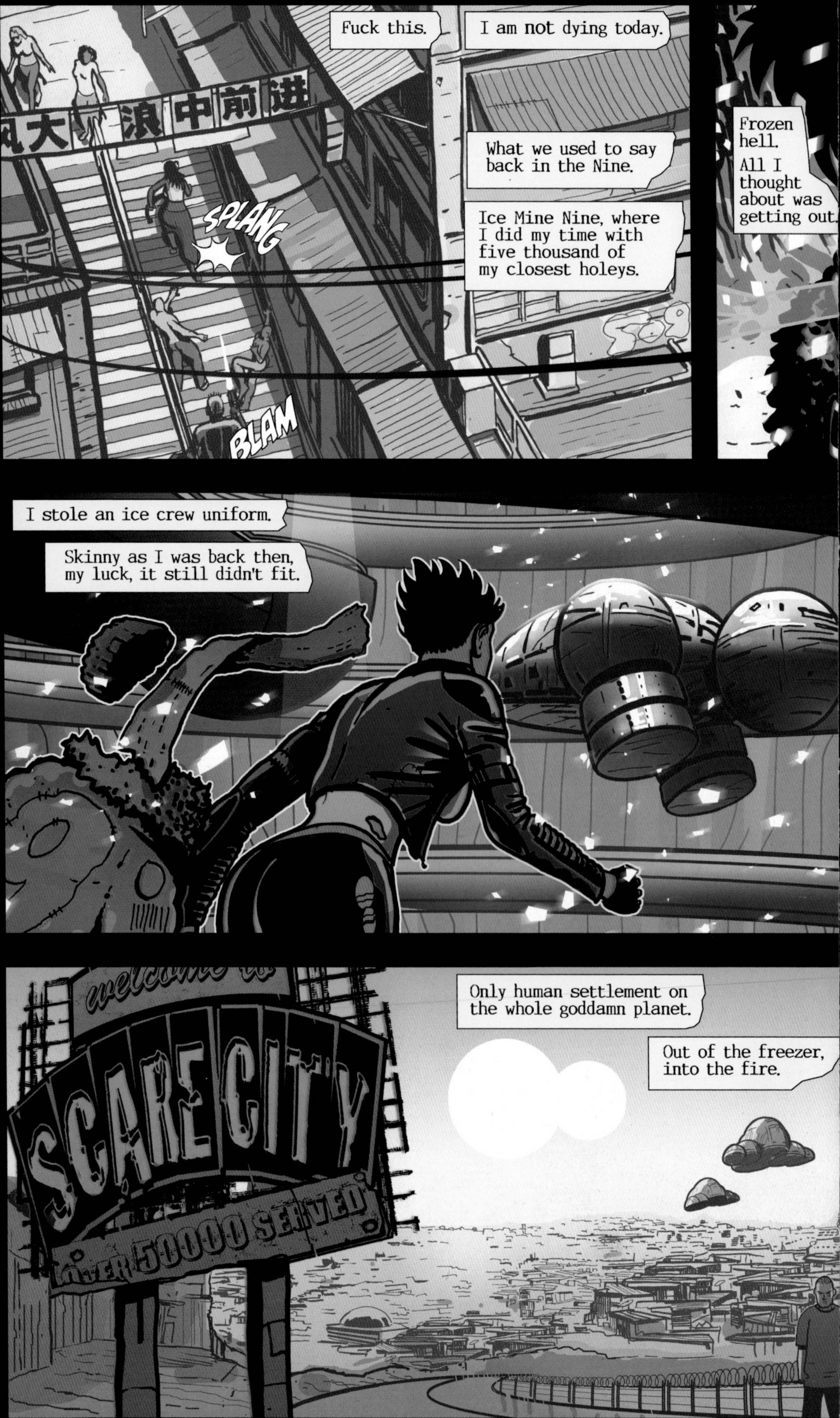

Fuck this.
I am not dying today.
大浪中前进
What we used to say back in the Nine.
Ice Mine Nine, where I did my time with five thousand of my closest holeys.
SPLANG
BLAM
Frozen hell.
All I thought about was getting out.
I stole an ice crew uniform.
Skinny as I was back then, my luck, it still didn't fit.
SCARE CITY
OVER 50000 SERVED
Only human settlement on the whole goddamn planet.
Out of the freezer, into the fire.

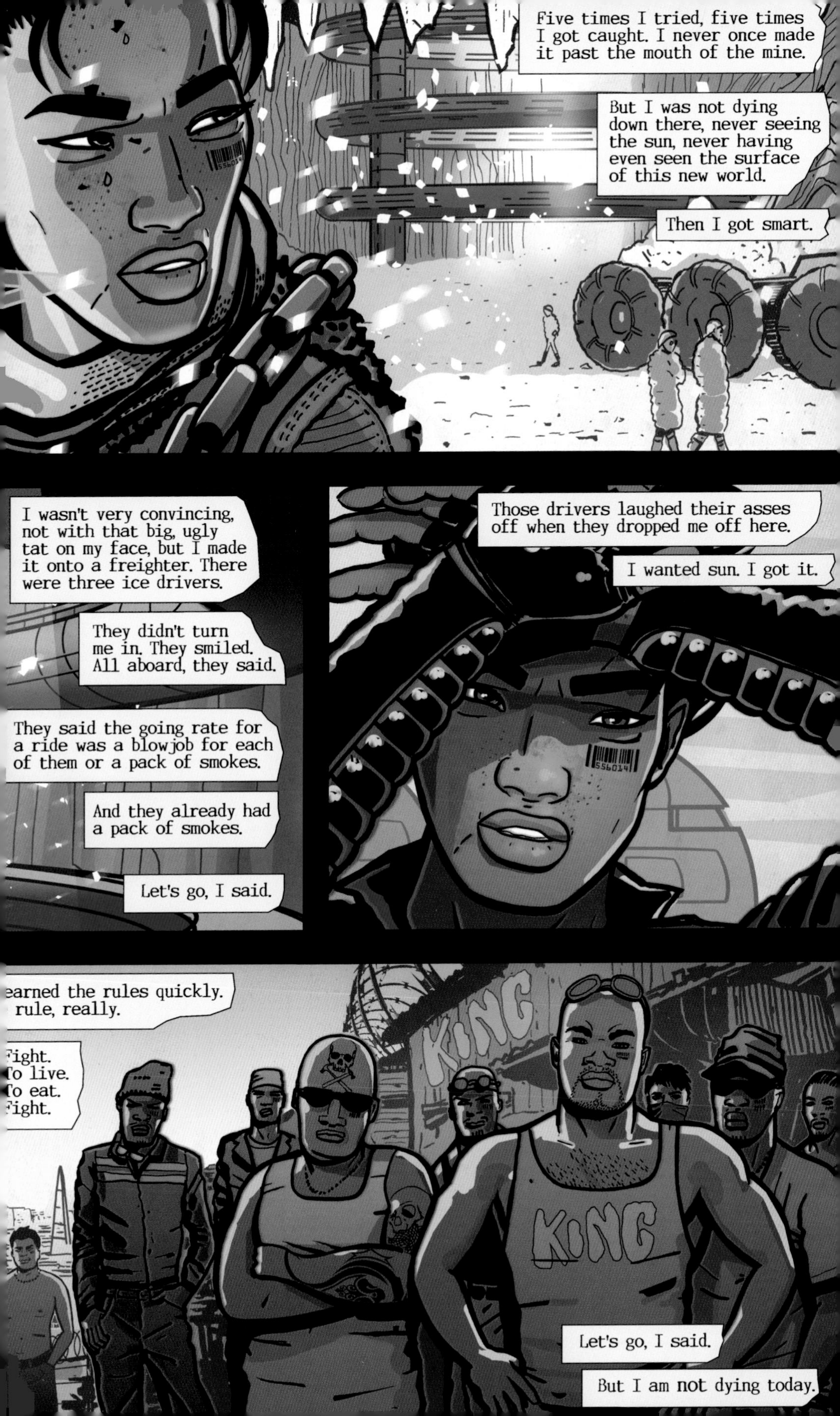
Five times I tried, five times I got caught. I never once made it past the mouth of the mine.
But I was not dying down there, never seeing the sun, never having even seen the surface of this new world.
Then I got smart.
I wasn't very convincing, not with that big, ugly tat on my face, but I made it onto a freighter. There were three ice drivers.
They didn't turn me in. They smiled. All aboard, they said.
They said the going rate for a ride was a blowjob for each of them or a pack of smokes.
And they already had a pack of smokes.
Let's go, I said.
Those drivers laughed their asses off when they dropped me off here.
I wanted sun. I got it.
earned the rules quickly.
rule, really.
Fight.
To live.
To eat.
Fight.
KING
KING
Let's go, I said.
But I am not dying today.

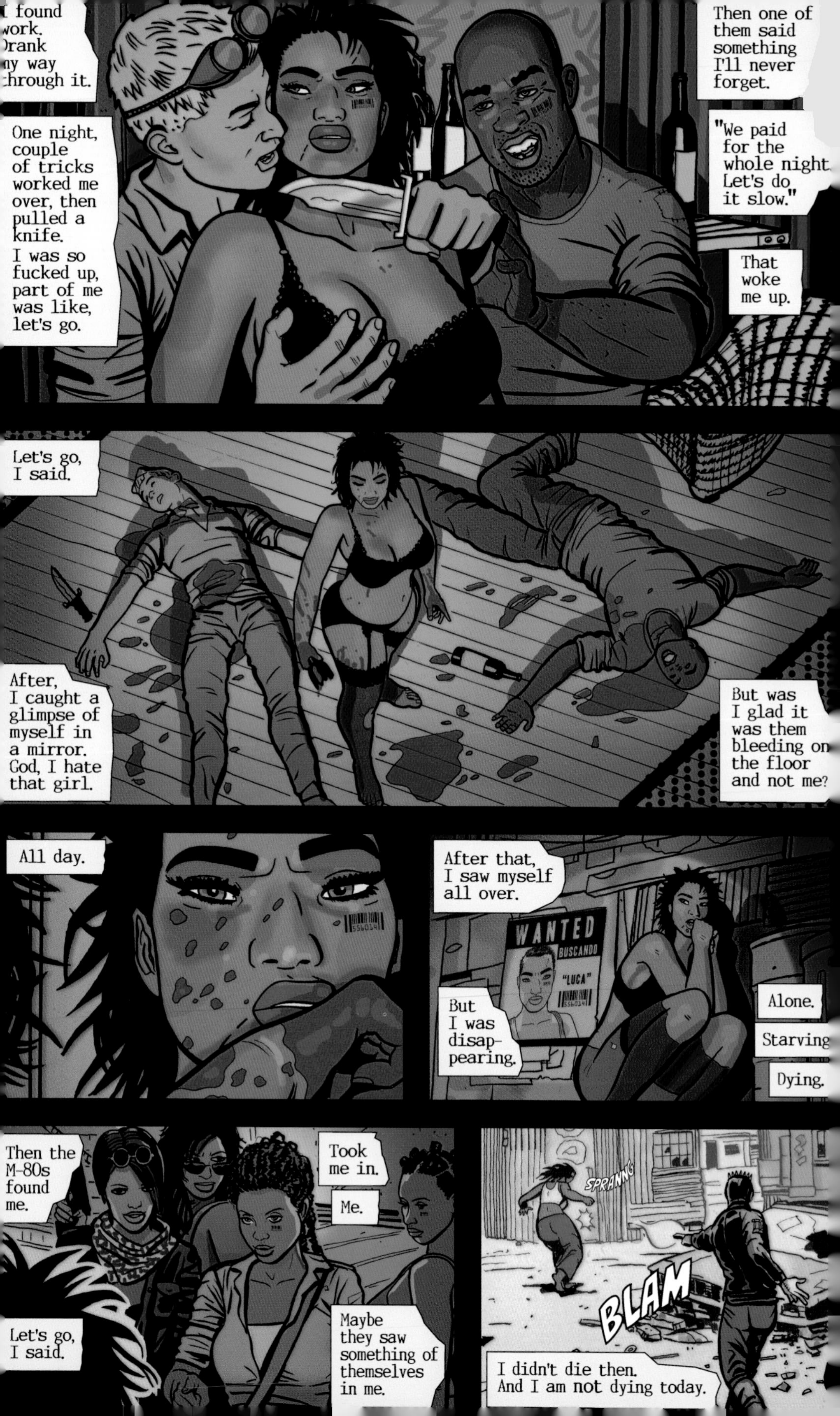
I found work. Drank my way through it.
One night, couple of tricks worked me over, then pulled a knife.
I was so fucked up, part of me was like, let's go.
Then one of them said something I'll never forget.
"We paid for the whole night. Let's do it slow."
That woke me up.
Let's go, I said.
After, I caught a glimpse of myself in a mirror. God, I hate that girl.
But was I glad it was them bleeding on the floor and not me?
All day.
After that, I saw myself all over.
WANTED
BUSCANDO
"LUCA"
556014
But I was disap-pearing.
Alone.
Starving.
Dying.
Then the M-80s found me.
Took me in.
Me.
Let's go, I said.
Maybe they saw something of themselves in me.
SPRANNG
BLAM
I didn't die then. And I am not dying today.

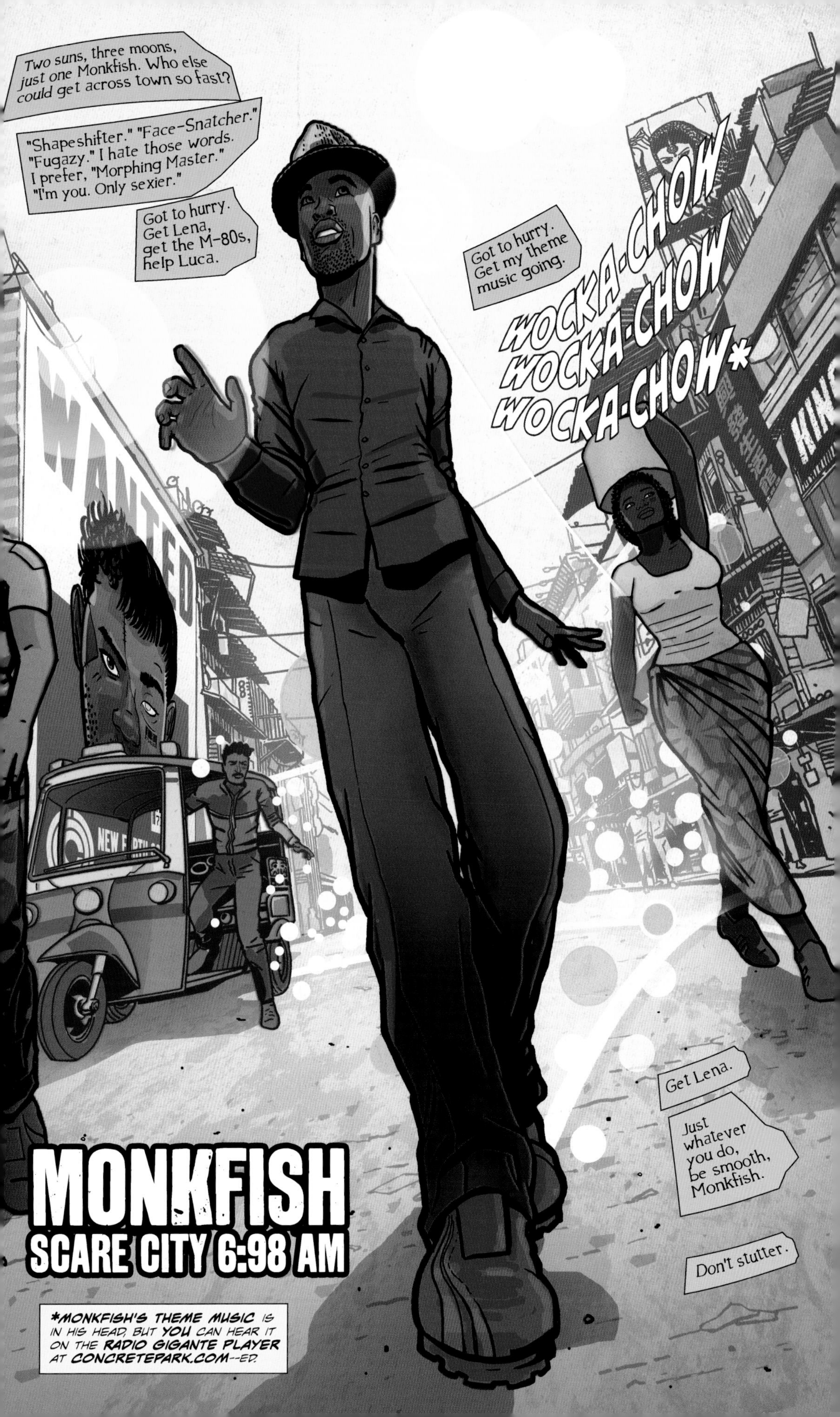
Two suns, three moons, just one Monkfish. Who else could get across town so fast?
"Shapeshifter." "Face-Snatcher." "Fugazy." I hate those words. I prefer, "Morphing Master." "I'm you. Only sexier."
Got to hurry. Get Lena, get the M-80s, help Luca.
Got to hurry. Get my theme music going.
WOCKA-CHOW WOCKA-CHOW WOCKA-CHOW*
Get Lena.
Just whatever you do, be smooth, Monkfish.
Don't stutter.
MONKFISH
SCARE CITY 6:98 AM
*MONKFISH'S THEME MUSIC IS IN HIS HEAD, BUT YOU CAN HEAR IT ON THE RADIO GIGANTE PLAYER AT CONCRETEPARK.COM--ED.

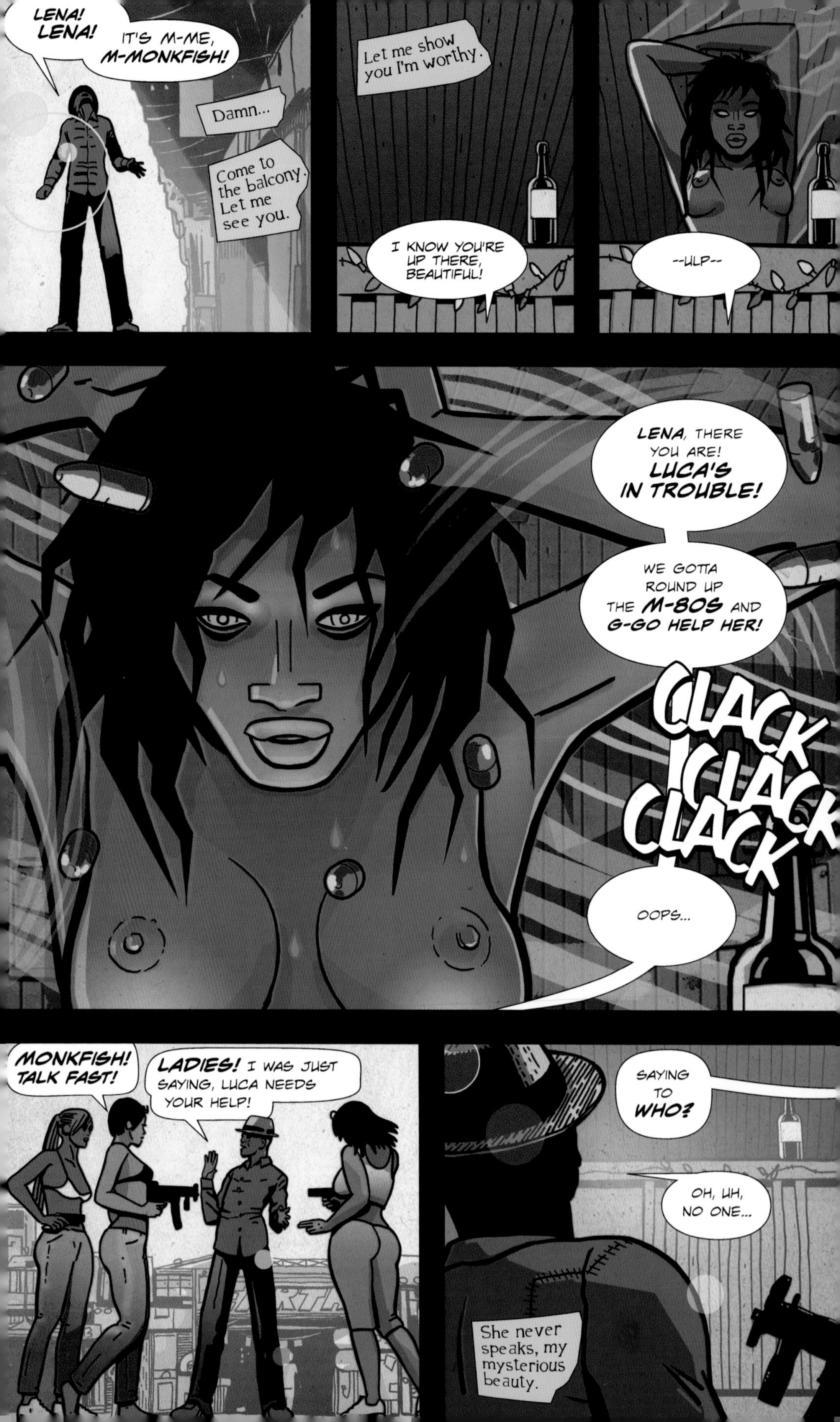
LENA! LENA!
IT'S M-ME, M-MONKFISH!
Damn...
Come to the balcony. Let me see you.
Let me show you I'm worthy.
I KNOW YOU'RE UP THERE, BEAUTIFUL!
--ULP--
LENA, THERE YOU ARE! LUCA'S IN TROUBLE!
WE GOTTA ROUND UP THE M-80S AND G-GO HELP HER!
CLACK CLACK CLACK
OOPS...
MONKFISH! TALK FAST!
LADIES! I WAS JUST SAYING, LUCA NEEDS YOUR HELP!
SAYING TO WHO?
OH, UH, NO ONE...
She never speaks, my mysterious beauty.

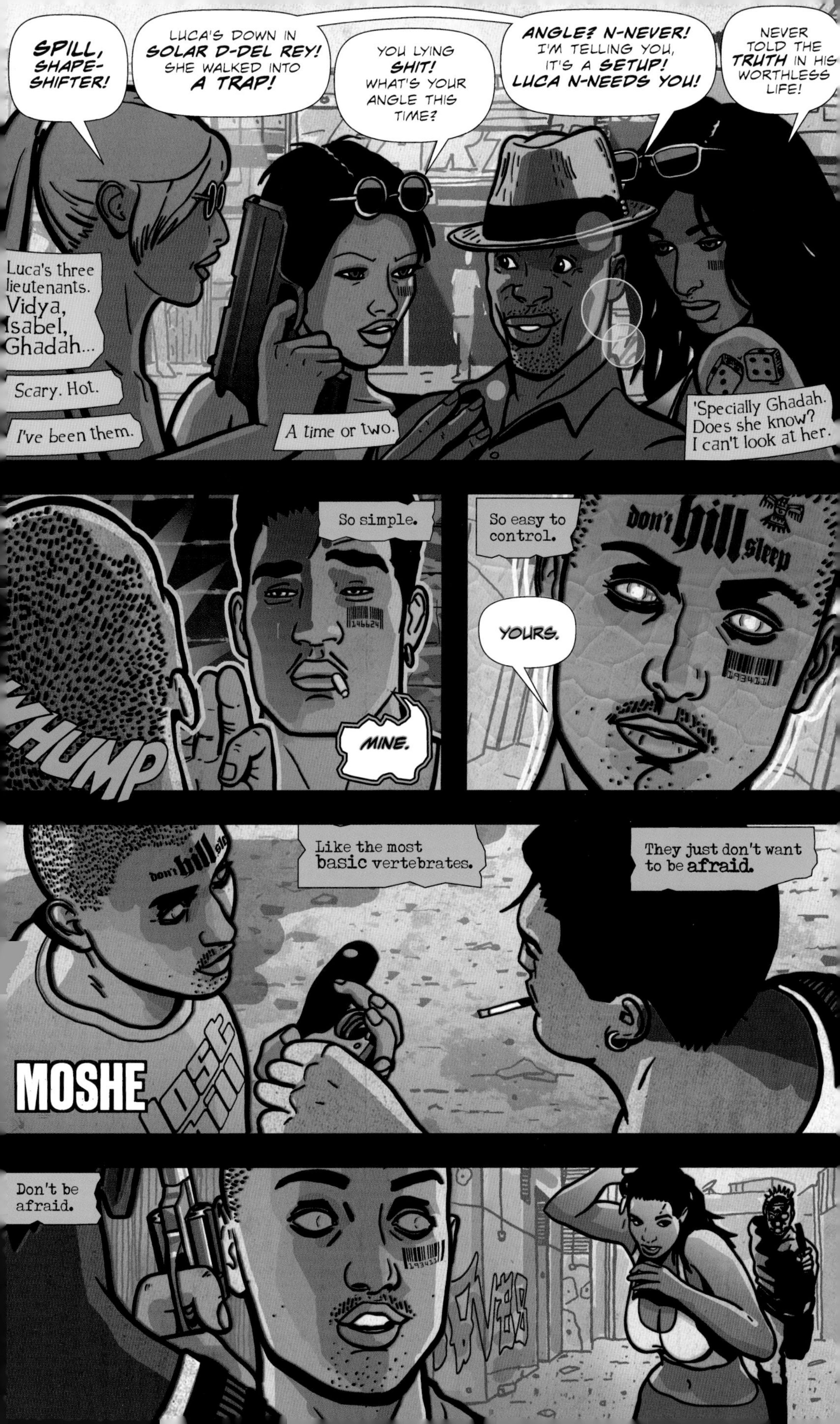
SPILL, SHAPE-SHIFTER!
LUCA'S DOWN IN SOLAR D-DEL REY! SHE WALKED INTO A TRAP!
YOU LYING SHIT! WHAT'S YOUR ANGLE THIS TIME?
ANGLE? N-NEVER! I'M TELLING YOU, IT'S A SETUP! LUCA N-NEEDS YOU!
NEVER TOLD THE TRUTH IN HIS WORTHLESS LIFE!
Luca's three lieutenants. Vidya, Isabel, Ghadah...
Scary. Hot.
I've been them.
A time or two.
'Specially Ghadah. Does she know? I can't look at her.
WHUMP
So simple.
MINE.
So easy to control.
YOURS.
Like the most basic vertebrates.
They just don't want to be afraid.
MOSHE
Don't be afraid.

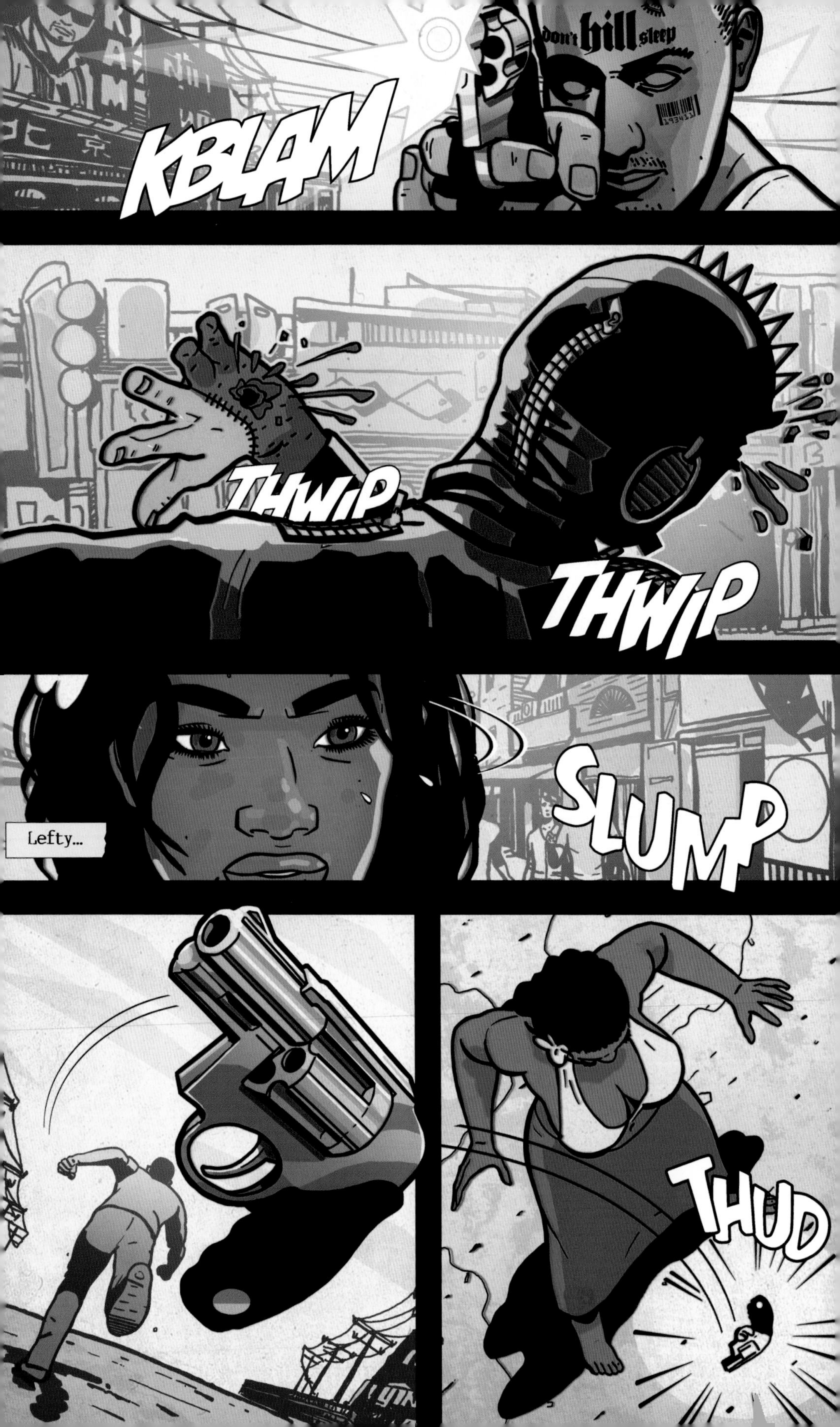

KBLAM
don't kill sleep
THWIP
THWIP
Lefty...
SLUMP
THUD

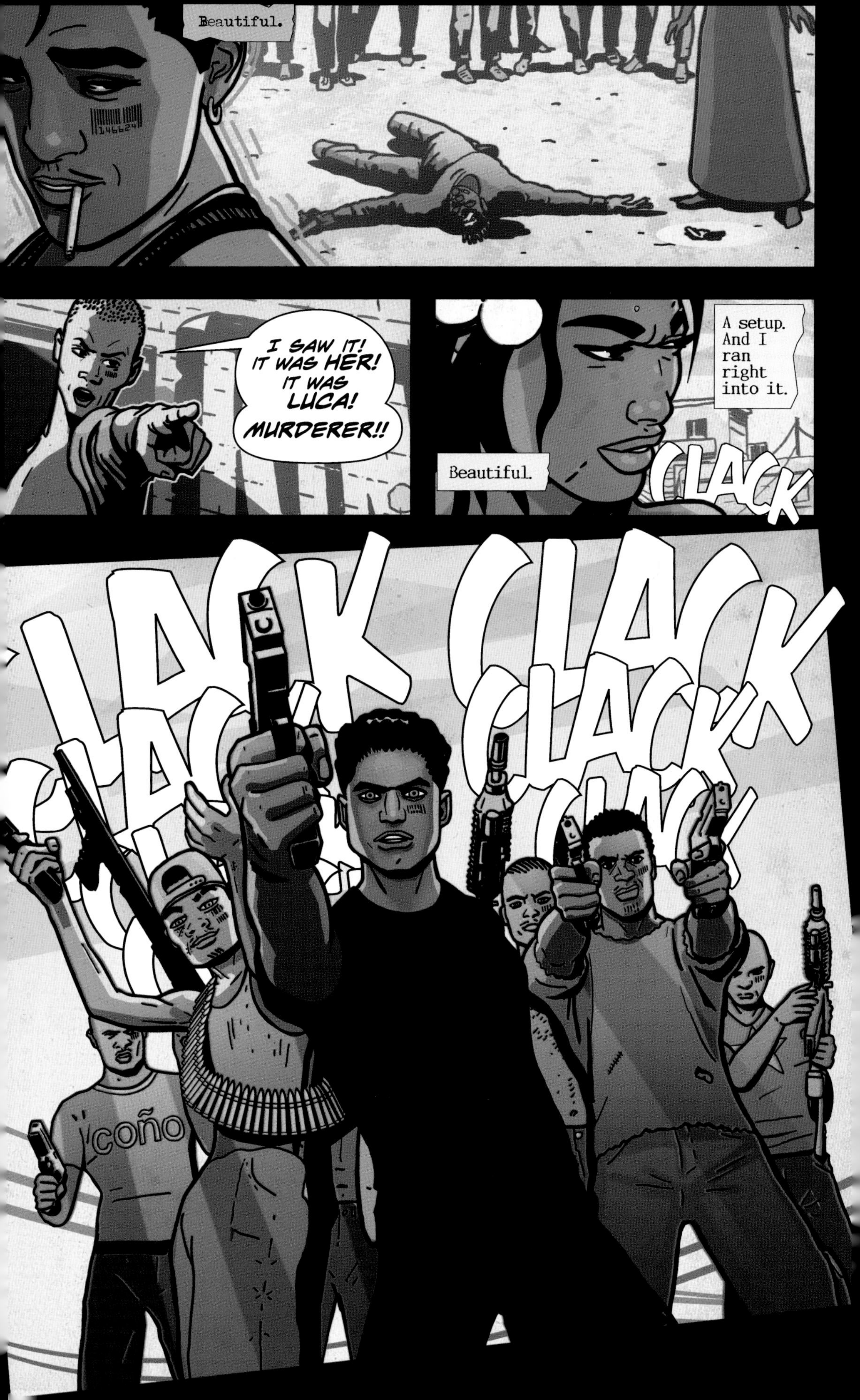
Beautiful.
146624
I SAW IT! IT WAS HER! IT WAS LUCA! MURDERER!!
A setup. And I ran right into it.
Beautiful.
CLACK
CLACK CLACK
CLACK
CLACK
coño

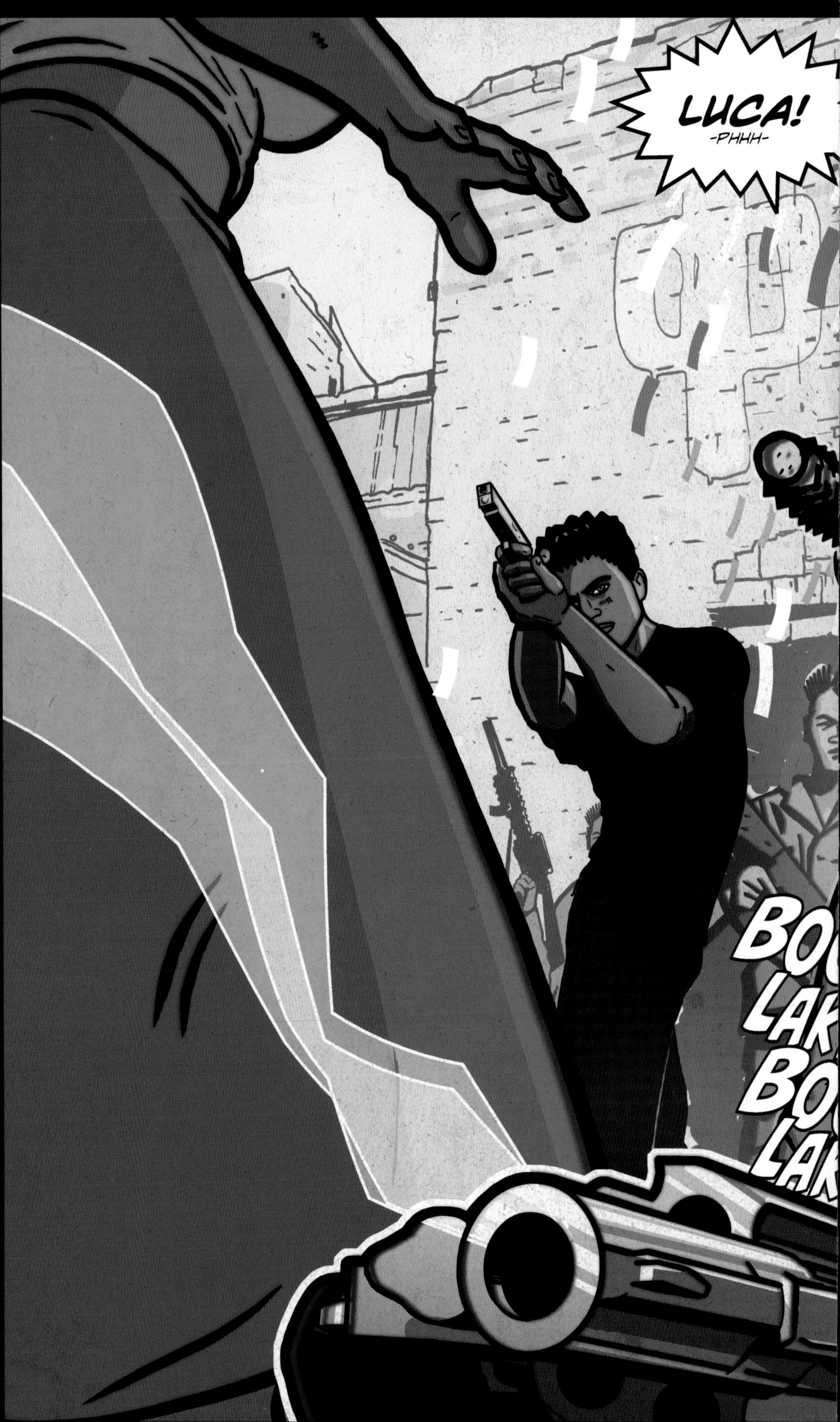
LUCA!
-PHHH-

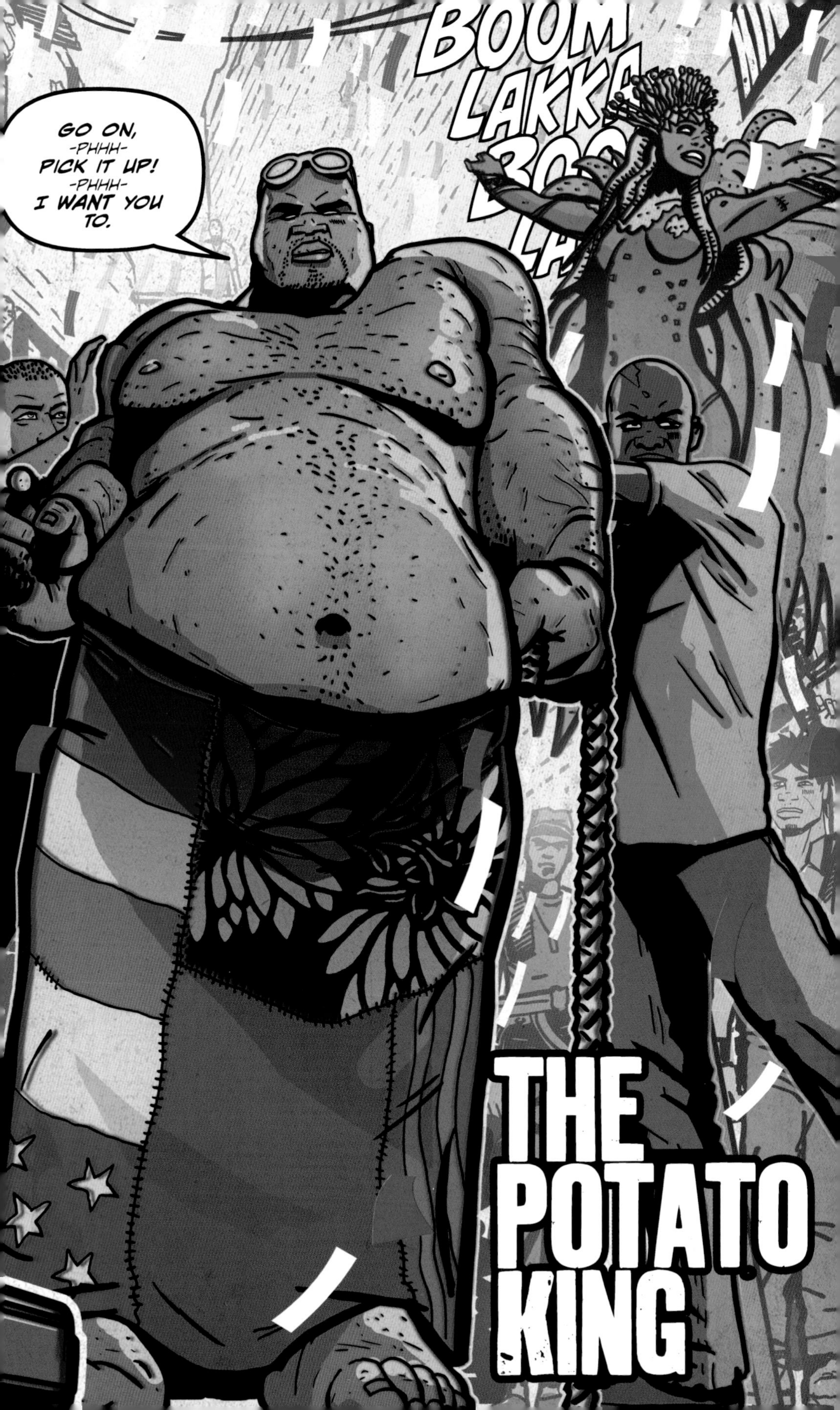
GO ON, -PHHH- PICK IT UP! -PHHH- I WANT YOU TO.
BOOM LAKKA BOO
THE POTATO KING

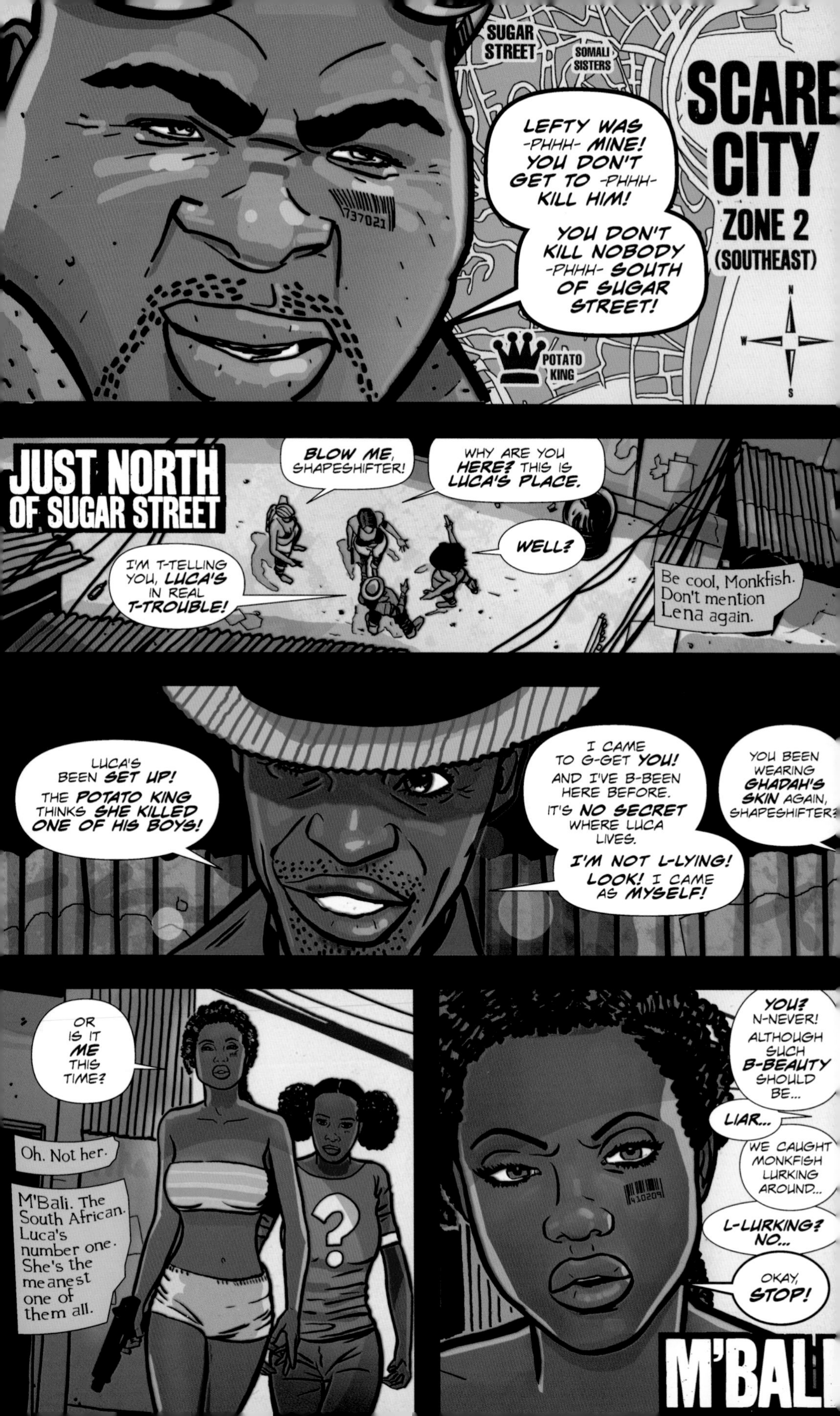
SUGAR STREET
SOMALI SISTERS
SCARE CITY ZONE 2 (SOUTHEAST)
LEFTY WAS -PHHH- MINE! YOU DON'T GET TO -PHHH- KILL HIM!
YOU DON'T KILL NOBODY -PHHH- SOUTH OF SUGAR STREET!
737021
N
W
S
POTATO KING
JUST NORTH OF SUGAR STREET
BLOW ME, SHAPESHIFTER!
WHY ARE YOU HERE? THIS IS LUCA'S PLACE.
WELL?
I'M T-TELLING YOU, LUCA'S IN REAL T-TROUBLE!
Be cool, Monkfish. Don't mention Lena again.
LUCA'S BEEN SET UP! THE POTATO KING THINKS SHE KILLED ONE OF HIS BOYS!
I CAME TO G-GET YOU! AND I'VE B-BEEN HERE BEFORE. IT'S NO SECRET WHERE LUCA LIVES.
I'M NOT L-LYING! LOOK! I CAME AS MYSELF!
YOU BEEN WEARING GHADAH'S SKIN AGAIN, SHAPESHIFTER?
OR IS IT ME THIS TIME?
Oh. Not her.
M'Bali. The South African. Luca's number one. She's the meanest one of them all.
YOU? N-NEVER! ALTHOUGH SUCH B-BEAUTY SHOULD BE...
LIAR...
WE CAUGHT MONKFISH LURKING AROUND...
L-LURKING? NO...
OKAY, STOP!
410209
M'BALI

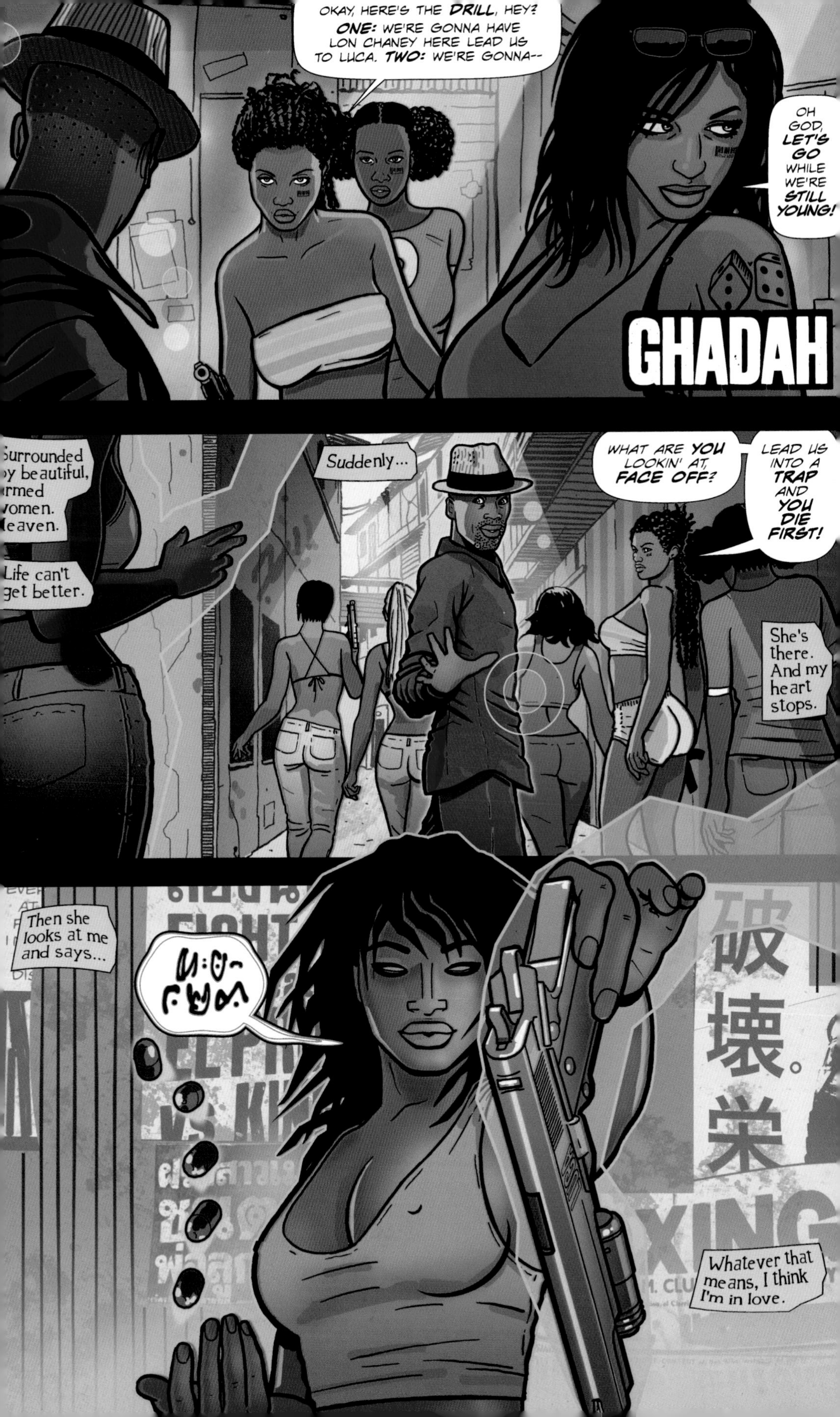
OKAY, HERE'S THE DRILL, HEY? ONE: WE'RE GONNA HAVE LON CHANEY HERE LEAD US TO LUCA. TWO: WE'RE GONNA--
OH GOD, LET'S GO WHILE WE'RE STILL YOUNG!
GHADAH
urrounded y beautiful, rmed omen. eaven.
Life can't get better.
Suddenly...
WHAT ARE YOU LOOKIN' AT, FACE OFF?
LEAD US INTO A TRAP AND YOU DIE FIRST!
She's there. And my heart stops.
Then she looks at me and says...
破壞。
XING
Whatever that means, I think I'm in love.

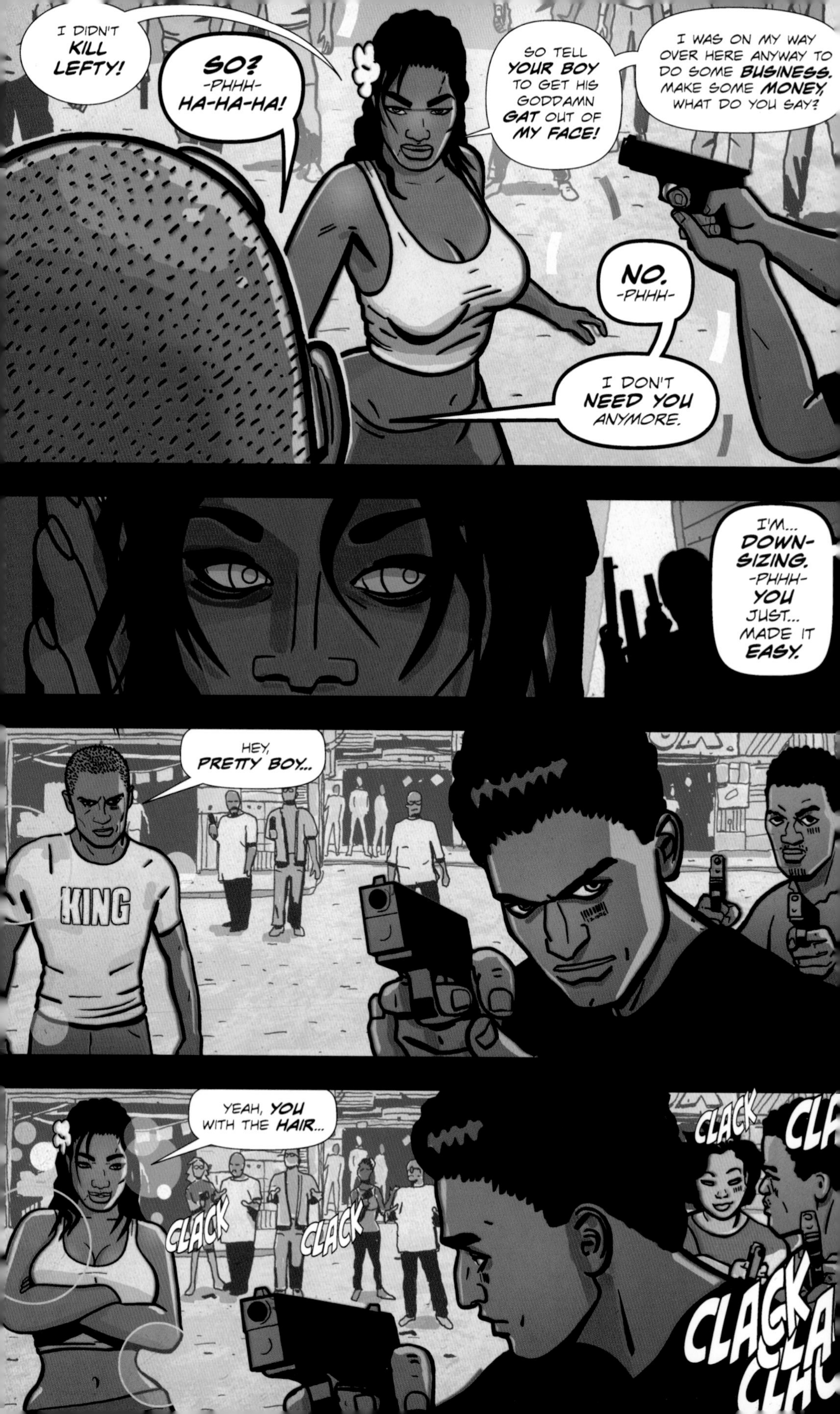
I DIDN'T KILL LEFTY!
SO? -PHHH- HA-HA-HA!
SO TELL YOUR BOY TO GET HIS GODDAMN GAT OUT OF MY FACE!
I WAS ON MY WAY OVER HERE ANYWAY TO DO SOME BUSINESS. MAKE SOME MONEY, WHAT DO YOU SAY?
NO. -PHHH-
I DON'T NEED YOU ANYMORE.
I'M... DOWN-SIZING. -PHHH- YOU JUST... MADE IT EASY.
HEY, PRETTY BOY...
KING
YEAH, YOU WITH THE HAIR...
CLACK
CLACK
CLACK
CLACK

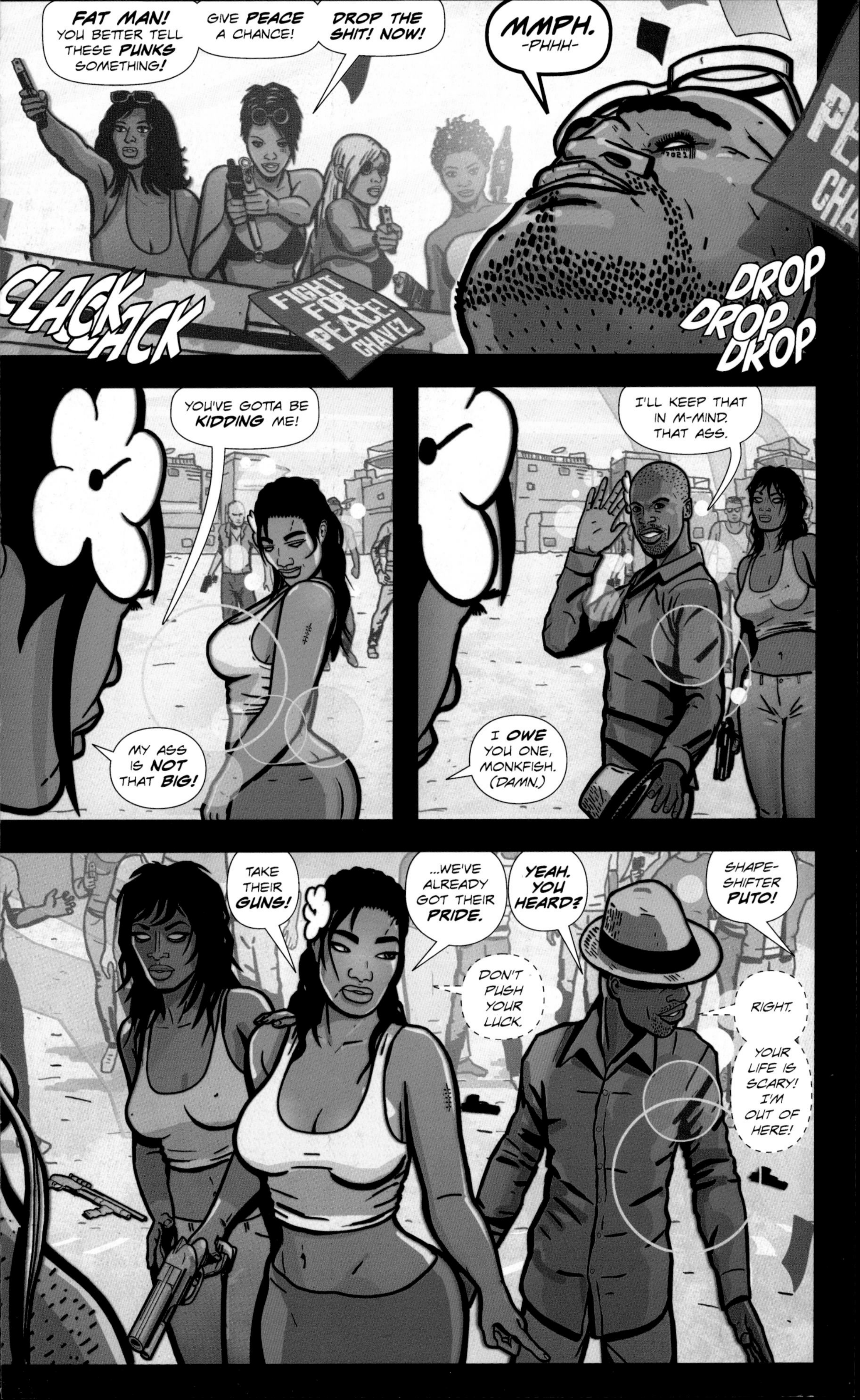
FAT MAN! YOU BETTER TELL THESE PUNKS SOMETHING!
GIVE PEACE A CHANCE!
DROP THE SHIT! NOW!
MMPH. -PHHH-
FIGHT FOR PEACE! CHAVEZ
CLACK CLACK
DROP DROP DROP
YOU'VE GOTTA BE KIDDING ME!
MY ASS IS NOT THAT BIG!
I'LL KEEP THAT IN M-MIND. THAT ASS.
I OWE YOU ONE, MONKFISH. (DAMN.)
TAKE THEIR GUNS!
...WE'VE ALREADY GOT THEIR PRIDE.
YEAH. YOU HEARD?
SHAPE-SHIFTER PUTO!
DON'T PUSH YOUR LUCK.
RIGHT.
YOUR LIFE IS SCARY! I'M OUT OF HERE!

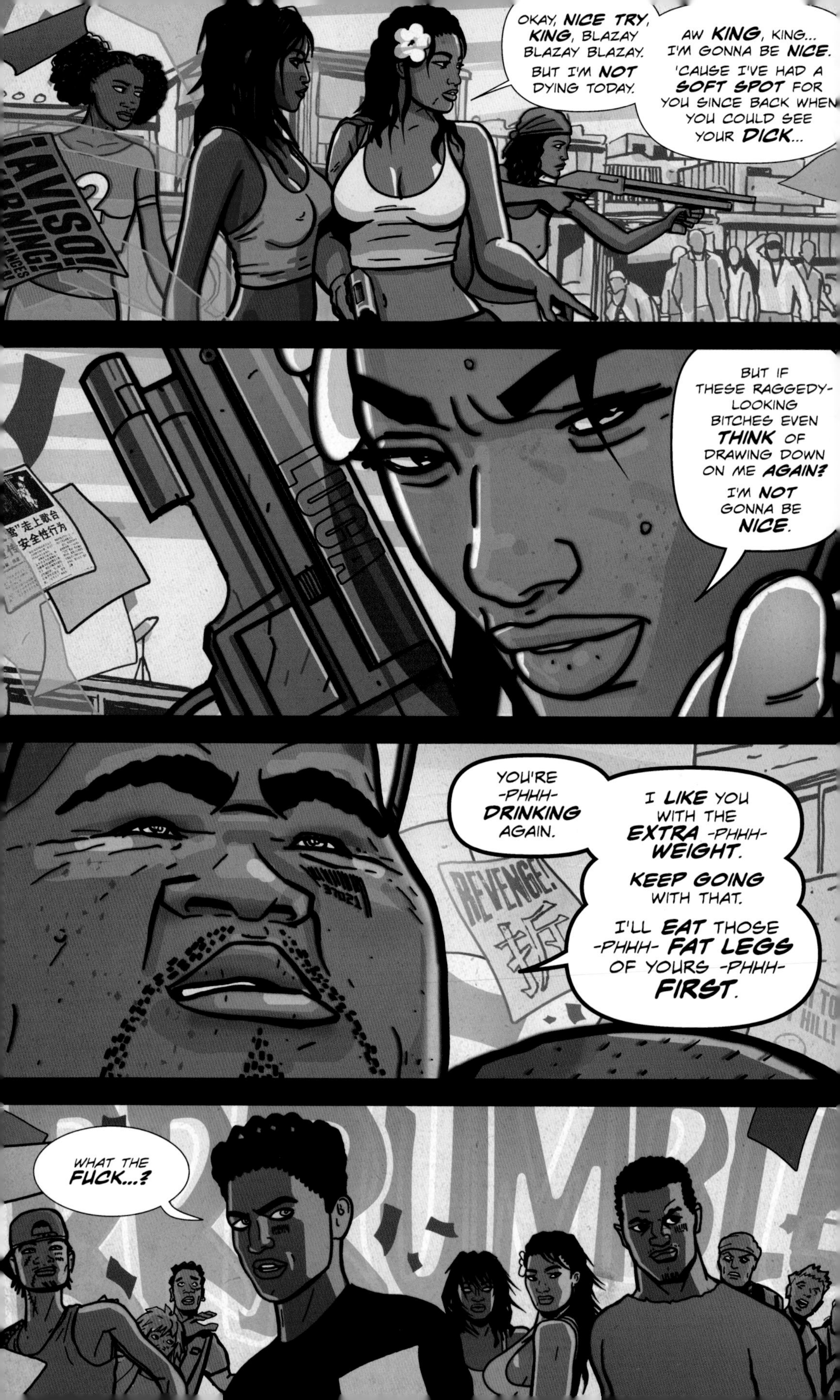

¡AVISO!
OKAY, NICE TRY, KING, BLAZAY BLAZAY BLAZAY. BUT I'M NOT DYING TODAY.
AW KING, KING... I'M GONNA BE NICE. 'CAUSE I'VE HAD A SOFT SPOT FOR YOU SINCE BACK WHEN YOU COULD SEE YOUR DICK...
BUT IF THESE RAGGEDY-LOOKING BITCHES EVEN THINK OF DRAWING DOWN ON ME AGAIN? I'M NOT GONNA BE NICE.
YOU'RE -PHHH- DRINKING AGAIN.
I LIKE YOU WITH THE EXTRA -PHHH- WEIGHT. KEEP GOING WITH THAT. I'LL EAT THOSE -PHHH- FAT LEGS OF YOURS -PHHH- FIRST.
REVENGE!
WHAT THE FUCK...?

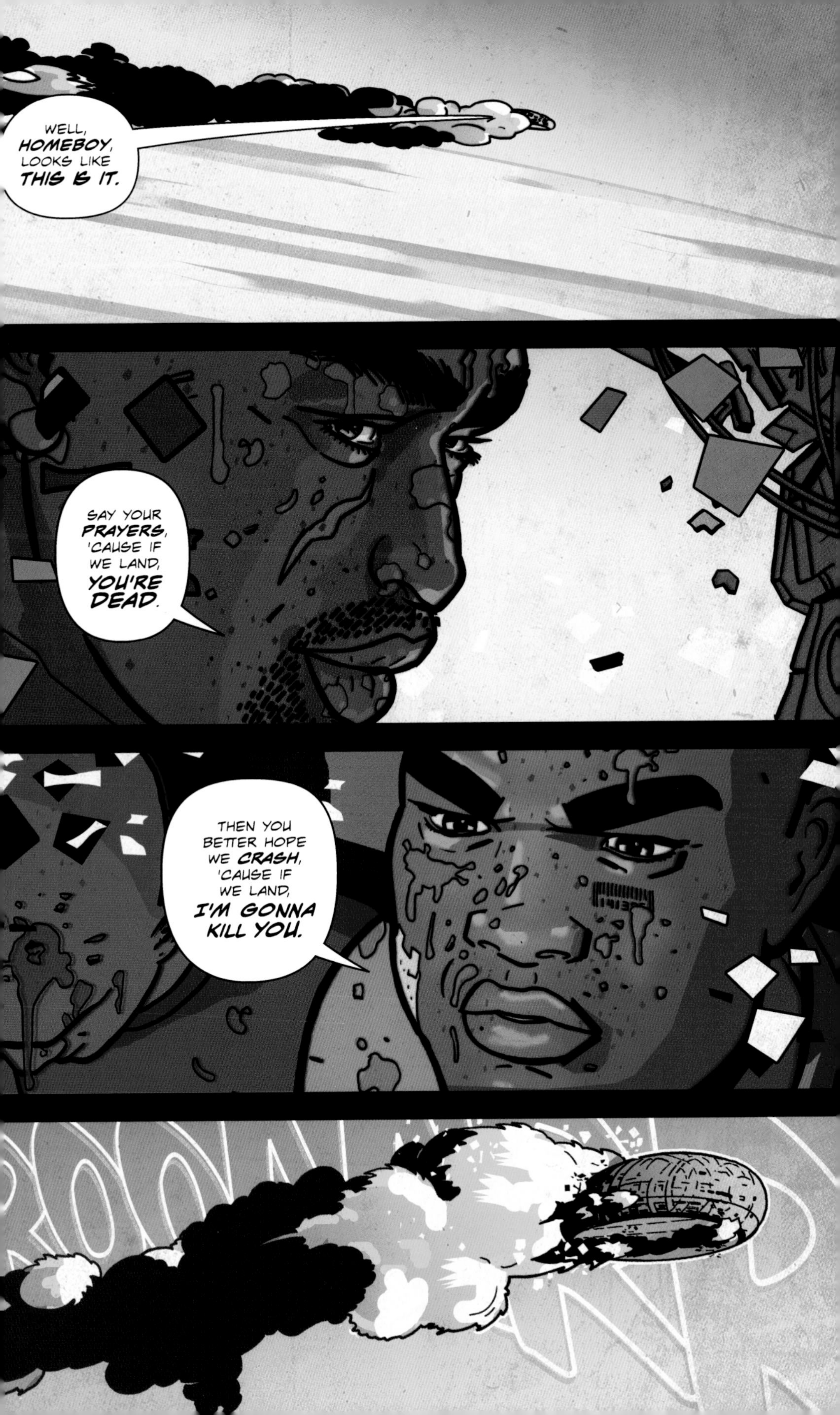
WELL, HOMEBOY, LOOKS LIKE THIS IS IT.
SAY YOUR PRAYERS, 'CAUSE IF WE LAND, YOU'RE DEAD.
THEN YOU BETTER HOPE WE CRASH, 'CAUSE IF WE LAND, I'M GONNA KILL YOU.

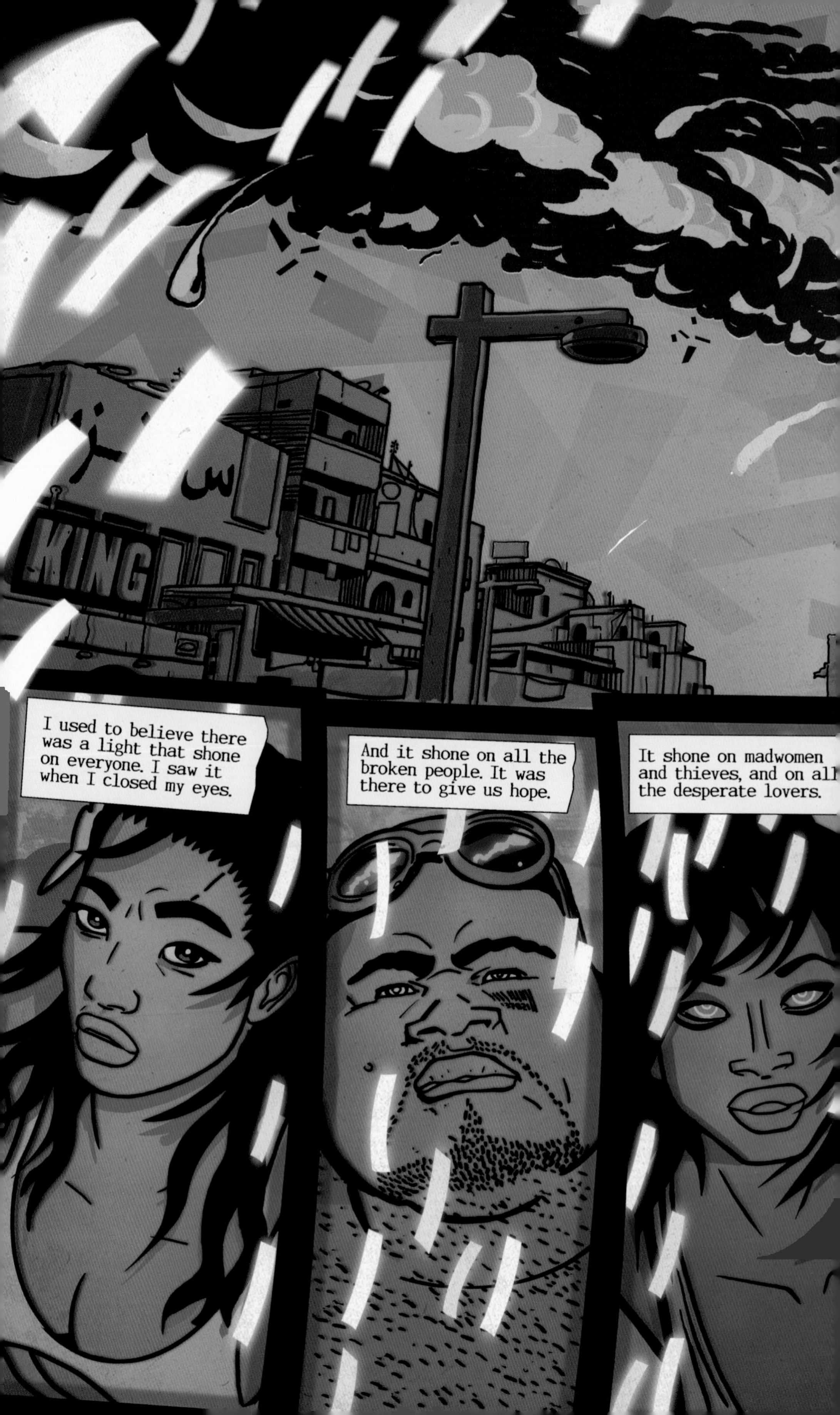
س
KING
I used to believe there was a light that shone on everyone. I saw it when I closed my eyes.
And it shone on all the broken people. It was there to give us hope.
It shone on madwomen and thieves, and on all the desperate lovers.

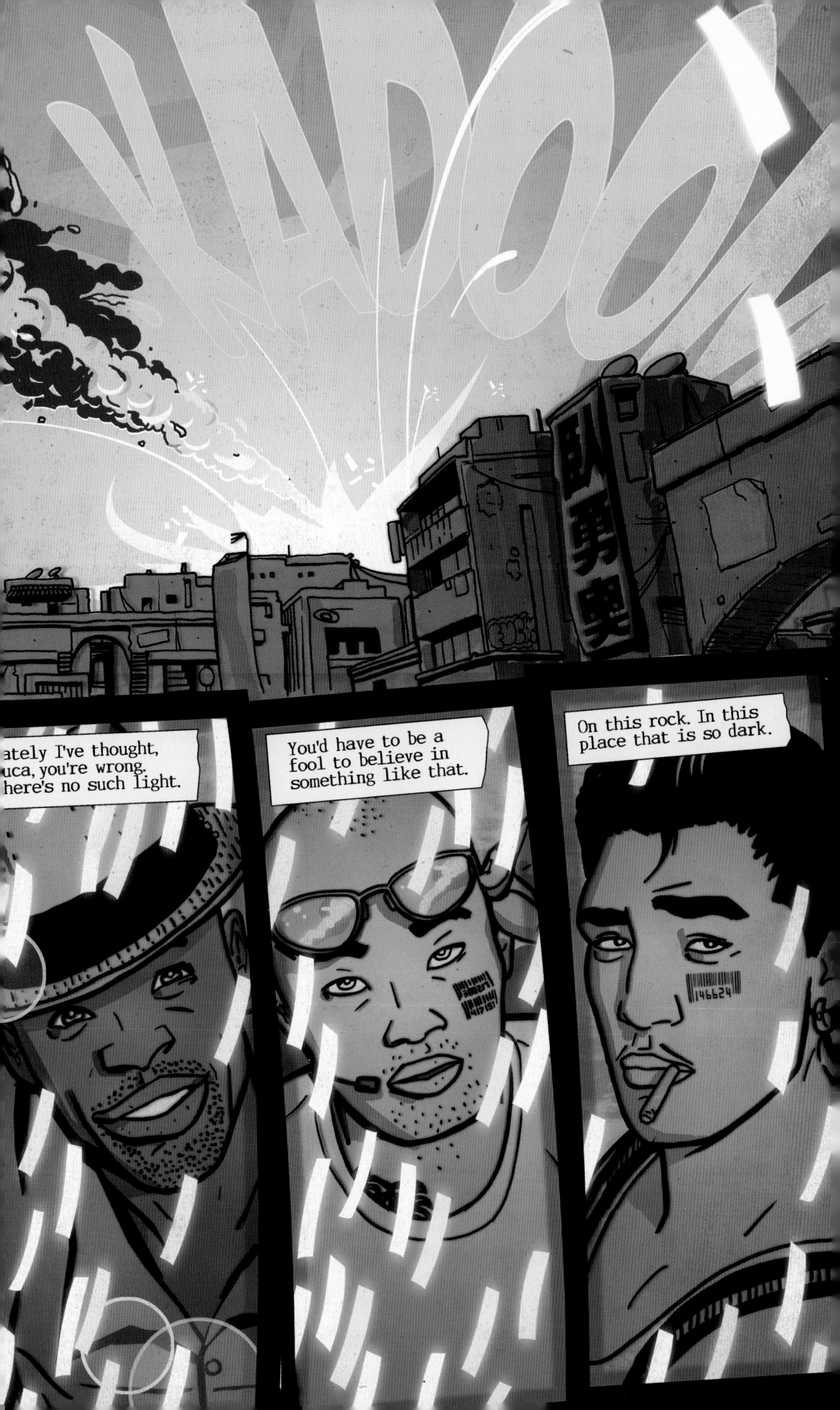
ately I've thought,
uca, you're wrong.
here's no such light.
You'd have to be a fool to believe in something like that.
On this rock. In this place that is so dark.

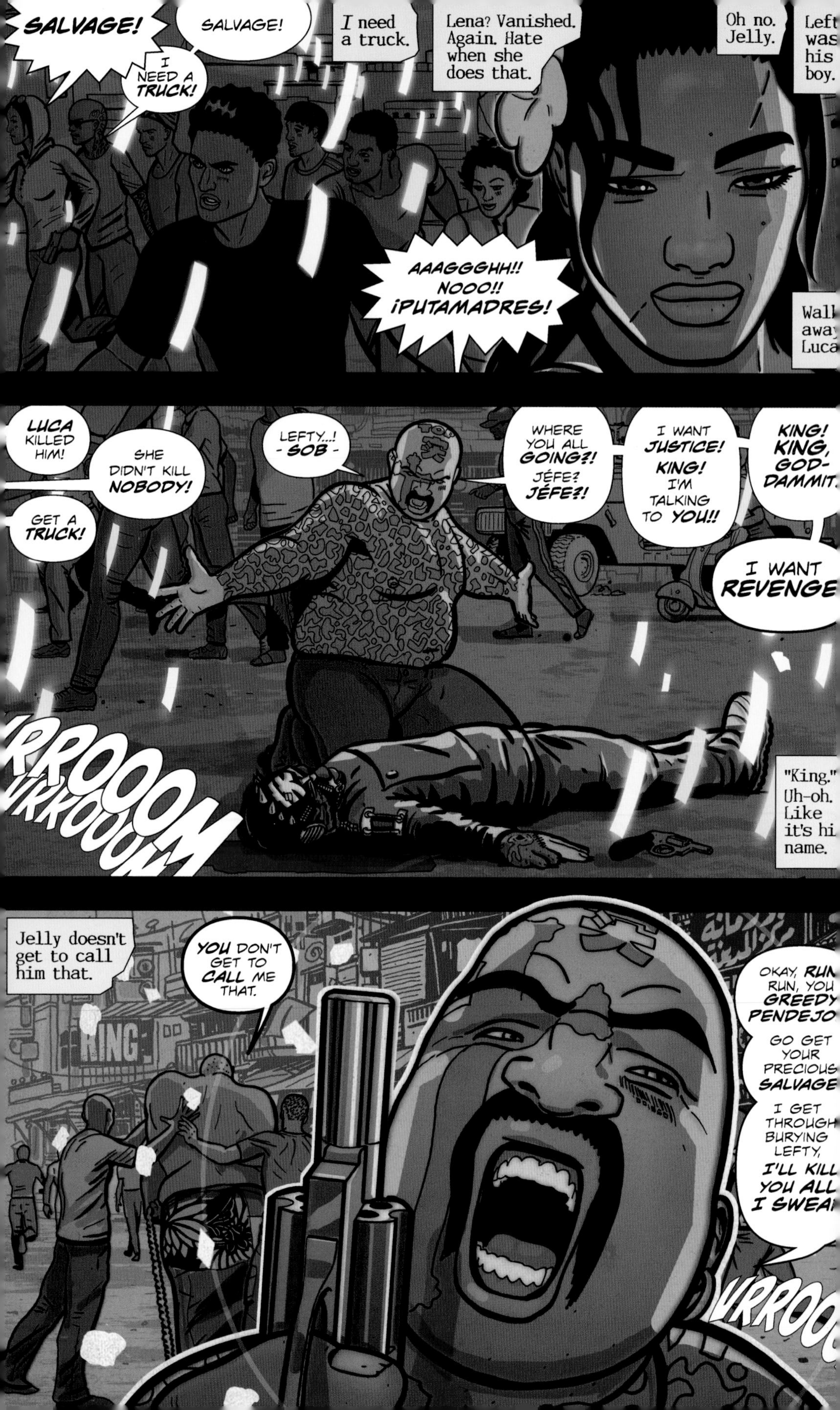
SALVAGE!
SALVAGE!
I NEED A TRUCK!
I need a truck.
Lena? Vanished. Again. Hate when she does that.
Oh no. Jelly.
Left was his boy.
AAAGGGHH!! NOOO!! ¡PUTAMADRES!
Wall away Luca
LUCA KILLED HIM!
SHE DIDN'T KILL NOBODY!
GET A TRUCK!
LEFTY...! - SOB -
WHERE YOU ALL GOING?! JÉFE? JÉFE?!
I WANT JUSTICE! KING! I'M TALKING TO YOU!!
KING! KING, GOD-DAMMIT.
I WANT REVENGE
VRROOOM VRROOOM
"King." Uh-oh. Like it's hi name.
Jelly doesn't get to call him that.
YOU DON'T GET TO CALL ME THAT.
KING
OKAY, RUN RUN, YOU GREEDY PENDEJO
GO GET YOUR PRECIOUS SALVAGE
I GET THROUGH BURYING LEFTY, I'LL KILL YOU ALL I SWEA
VRROO

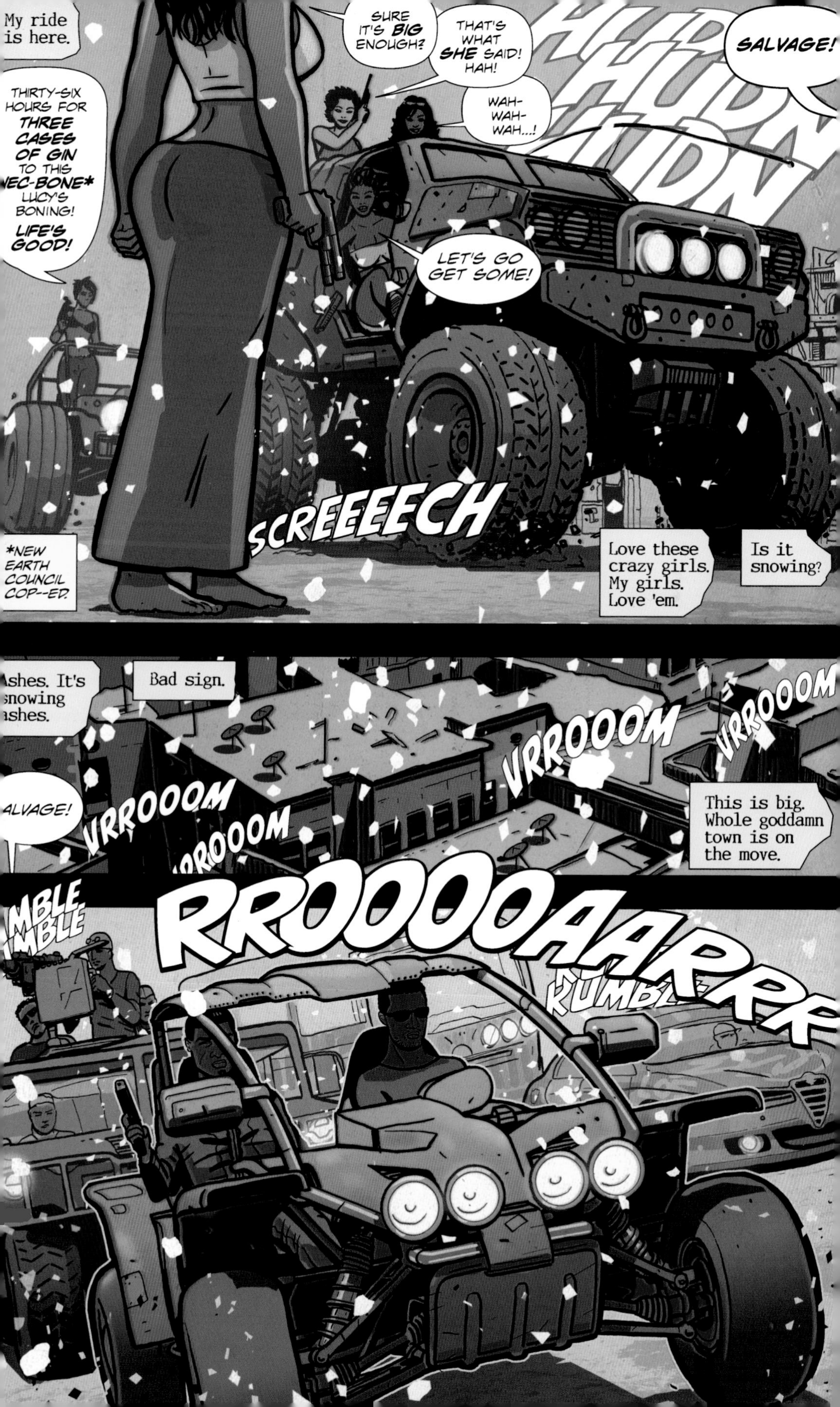
My ride is here.
SURE IT'S BIG ENOUGH?
THAT'S WHAT SHE SAID! HAH!
SALVAGE!
WAH-WAH-WAH...!
THIRTY-SIX HOURS FOR THREE CASES OF GIN TO THIS NEC-BONE* LUCY'S BONING! LIFE'S GOOD!
LET'S GO GET SOME!
SCREEEECH
*NEW EARTH COUNCIL COP--ED.
Love these crazy girls. My girls. Love 'em.
Is it snowing?
Ashes. It's snowing ashes.
Bad sign.
VRROOOM
VRROOOM
ALVAGE!
VRROOOM
ROOOM
This is big. Whole goddamn town is on the move.
RROOOOAARRR

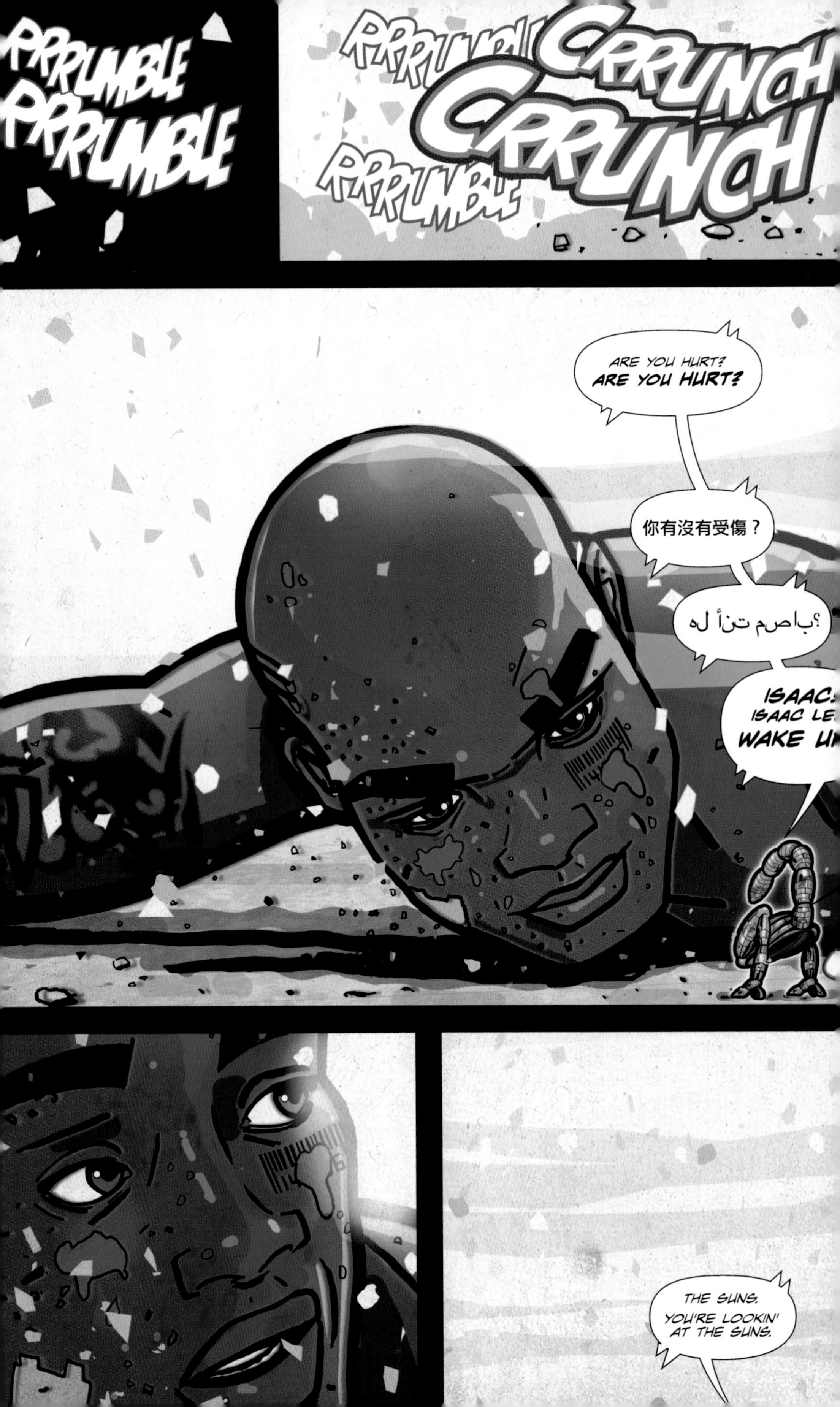
PRRUMBLE PRRUMBLE
RRRUMBLE CRRRUNCH CRRRUNCH RRRUMBLE
ARE YOU HURT? ARE YOU HURT?
你有沒有受傷？
هل أنت مصاب؟
THE SUNS. YOU'RE LOOKIN' AT THE SUNS.

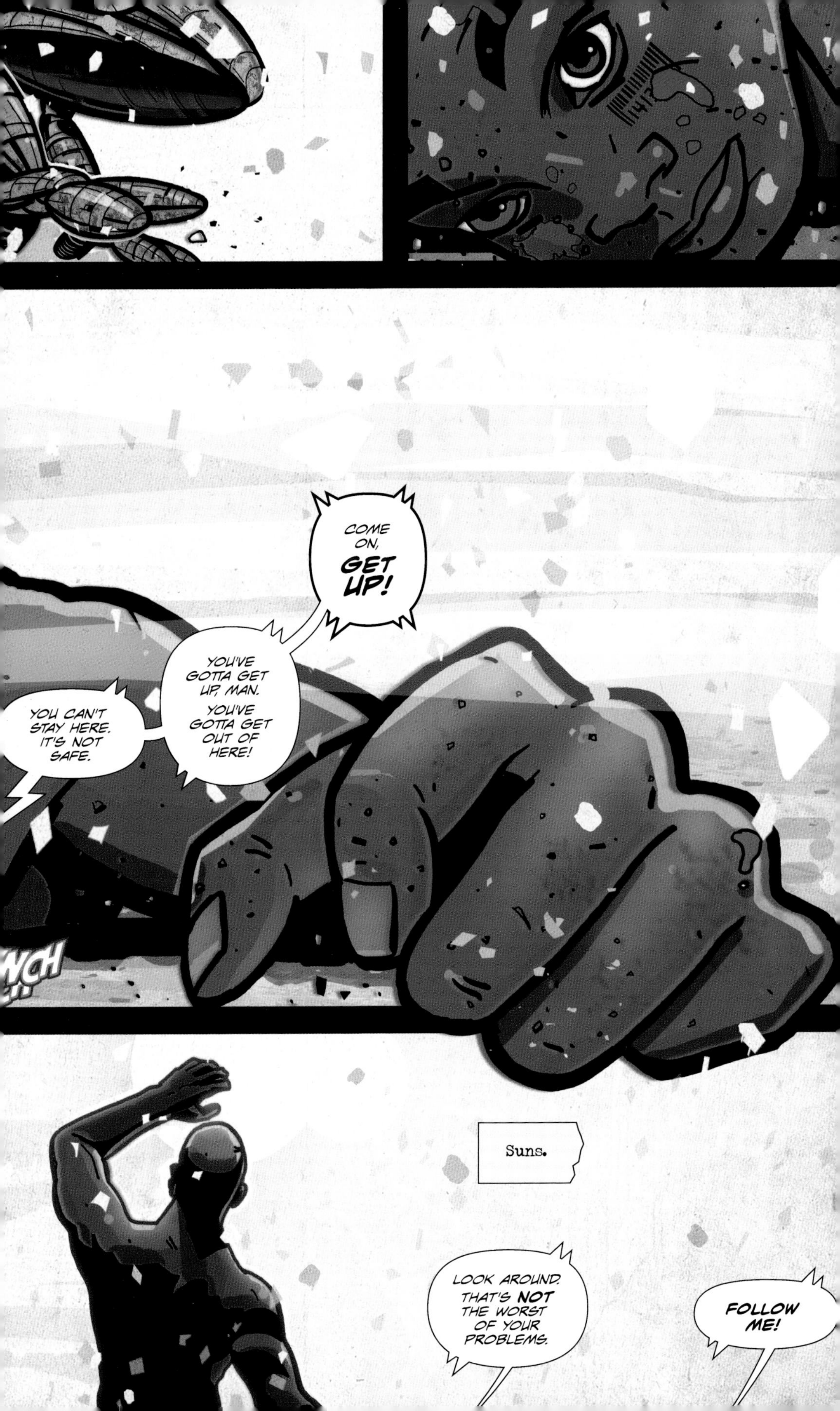
COME ON, GET UP!
YOU'VE GOTTA GET UP, MAN. YOU'VE GOTTA GET OUT OF HERE!
YOU CAN'T STAY HERE. IT'S NOT SAFE.
Suns.
LOOK AROUND. THAT'S NOT THE WORST OF YOUR PROBLEMS.
FOLLOW ME!

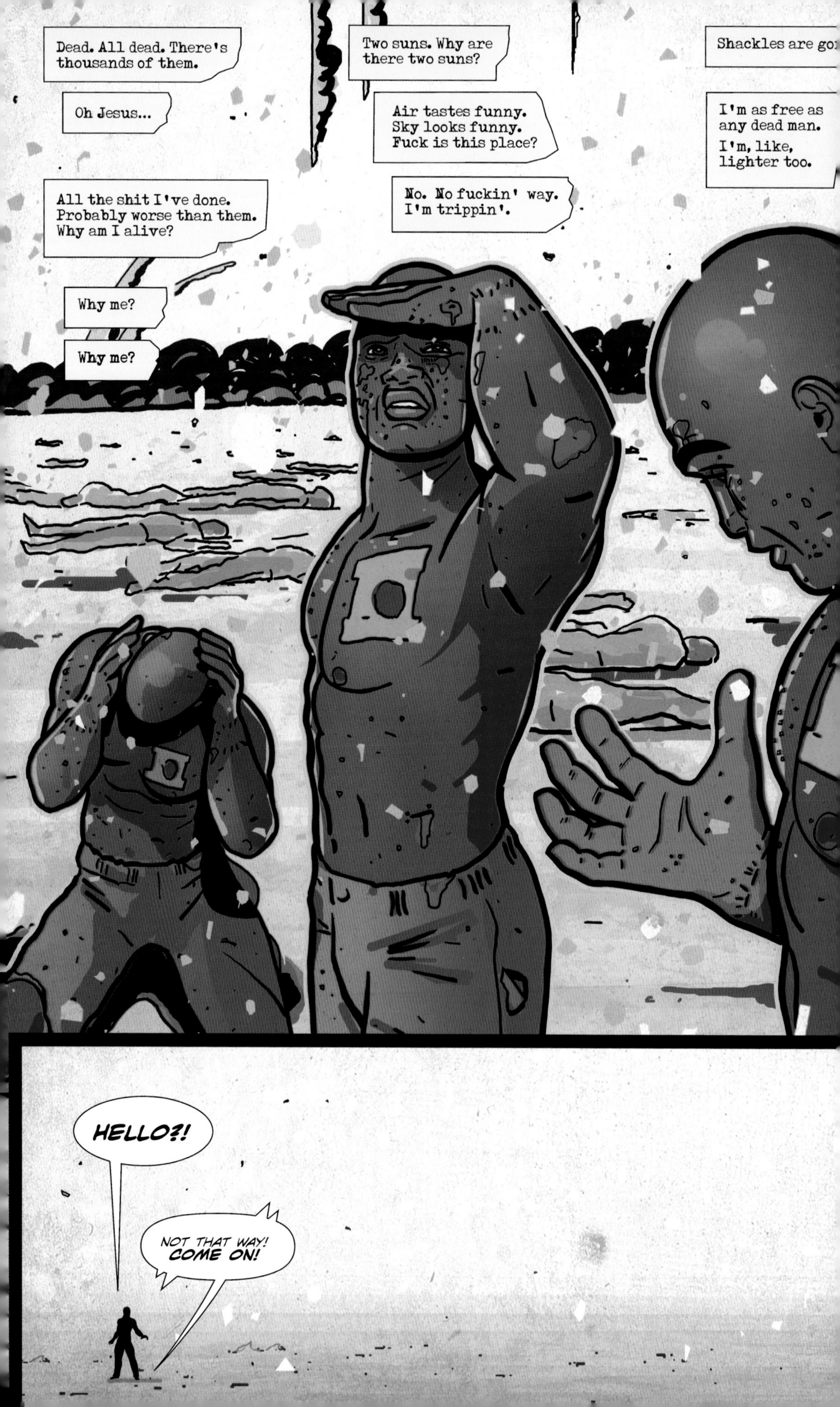

Dead. All dead. There's thousands of them.
Oh Jesus...
All the shit I've done. Probably worse than them. Why am I alive?
Why me?
Why me?
Two suns. Why are there two suns?
Air tastes funny. Sky looks funny. Fuck is this place?
No. No fuckin' way. I'm trippin'.
I'm as free as any dead man.
I'm, like, lighter too.
HELLO?!
NOT THAT WAY! COME ON!

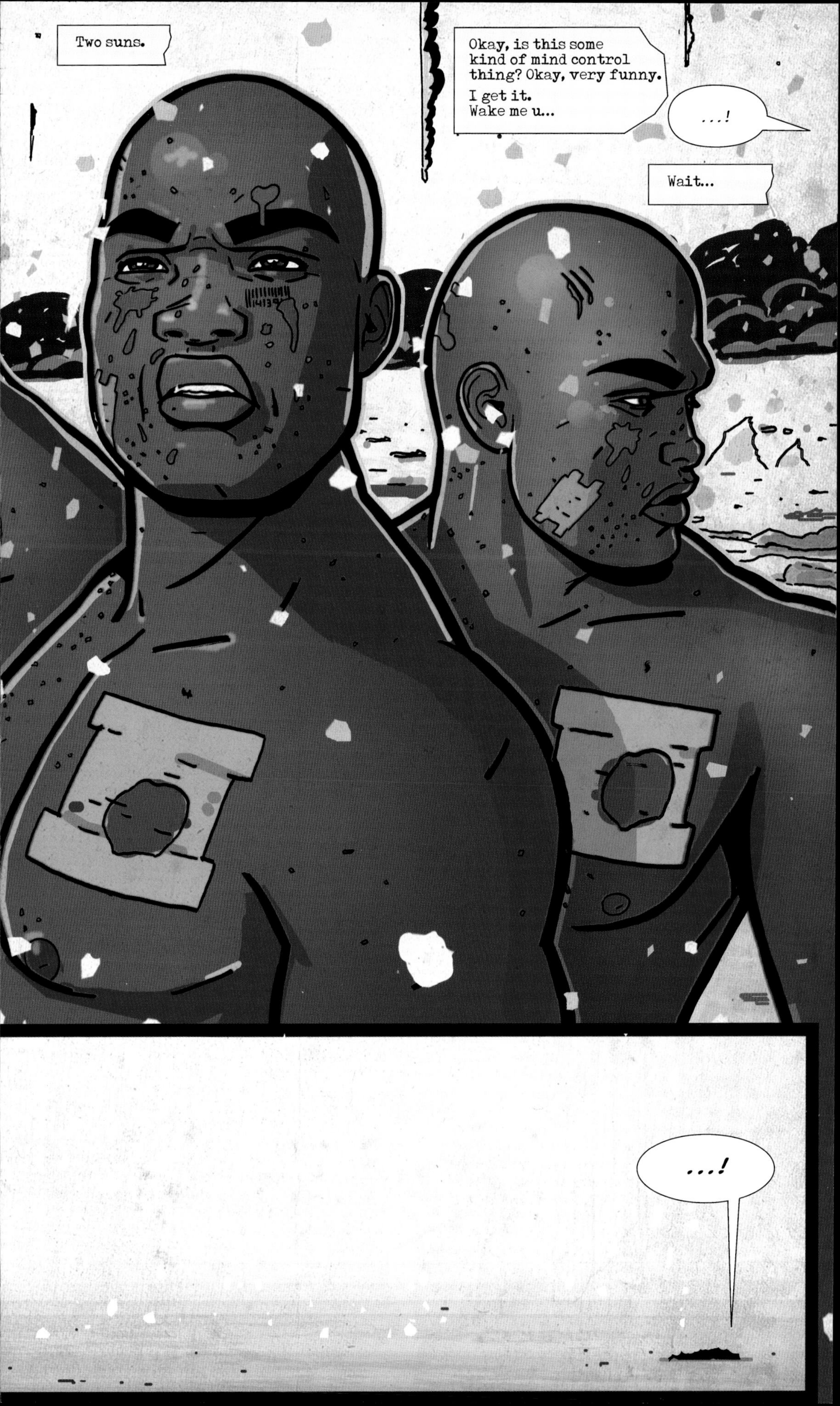
Two suns.
Okay, is this some kind of mind control thing? Okay, very funny.
I get it.
Wake me u...
...!
Wait...
...!

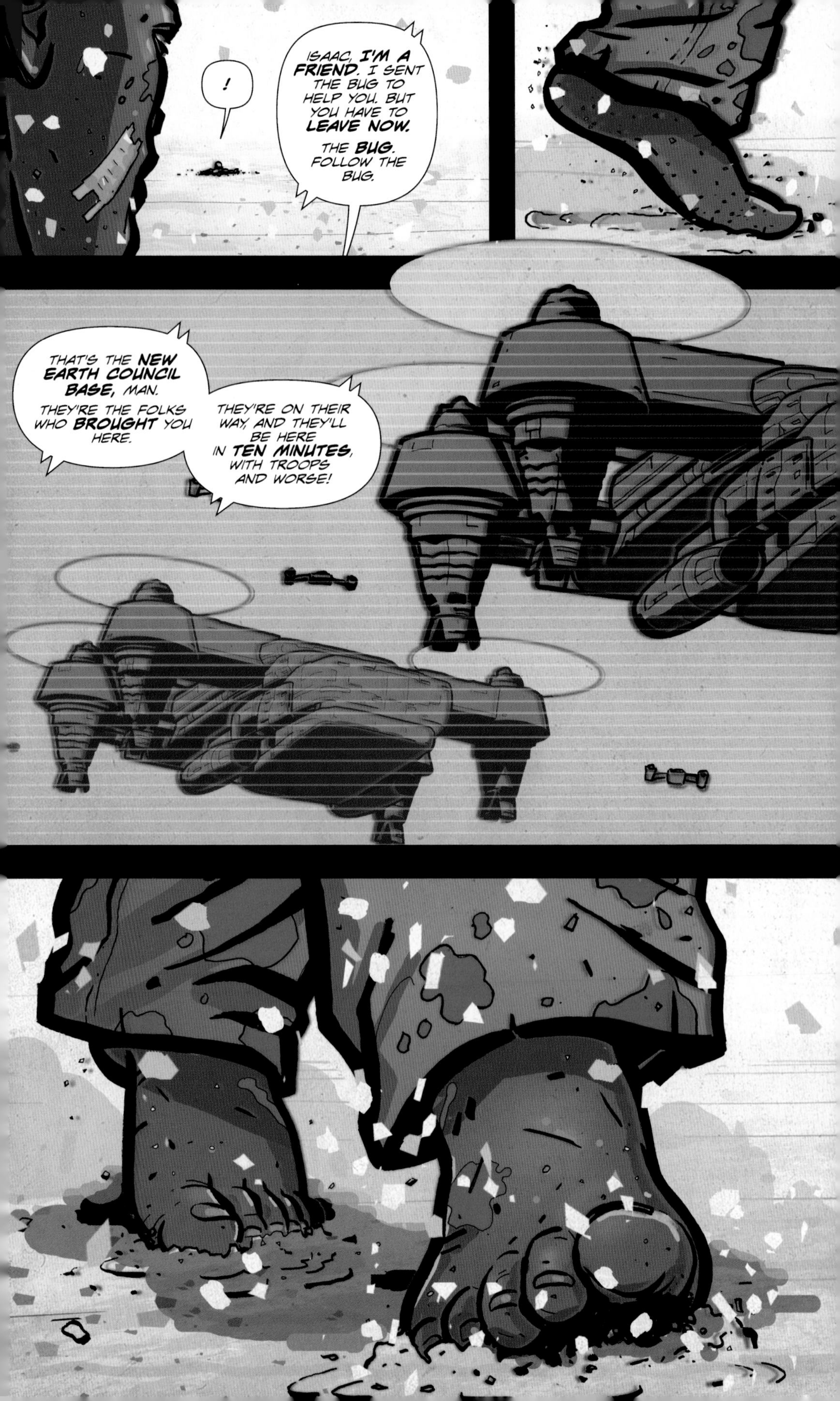
!
ISAAC, I'M A FRIEND. I SENT THE BUG TO HELP YOU. BUT YOU HAVE TO LEAVE NOW.
THE BUG. FOLLOW THE BUG.
THAT'S THE NEW EARTH COUNCIL BASE, MAN.
THEY'RE THE FOLKS WHO BROUGHT YOU HERE.
THEY'RE ON THEIR WAY, AND THEY'LL BE HERE IN TEN MINUTES, WITH TROOPS AND WORSE!

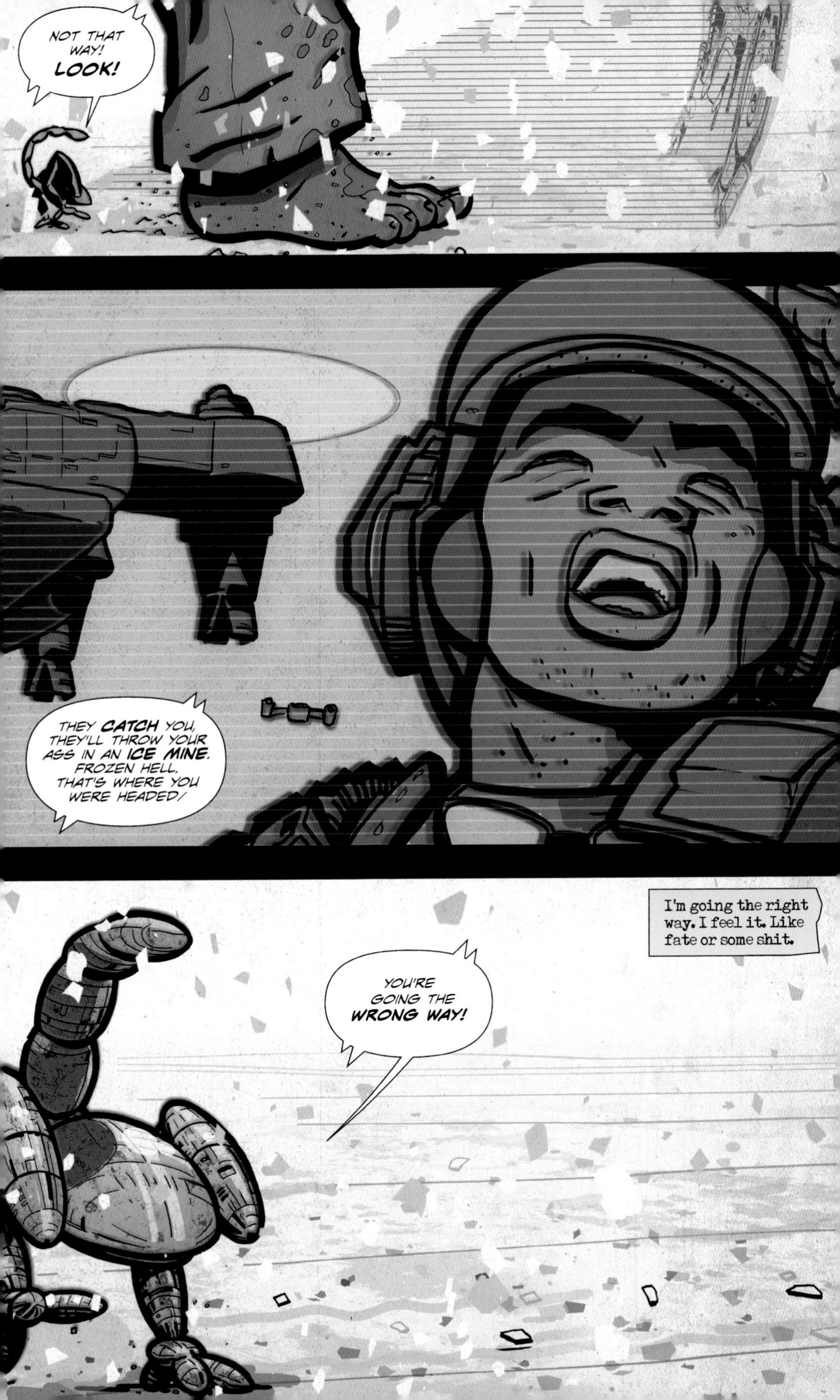

NOT THAT WAY! LOOK!
THEY CATCH YOU, THEY'LL THROW YOUR ASS IN AN ICE MINE. FROZEN HELL. THAT'S WHERE YOU WERE HEADED!
I'm going the right way. I feel it. Like fate or some shit.
YOU'RE GOING THE WRONG WAY!

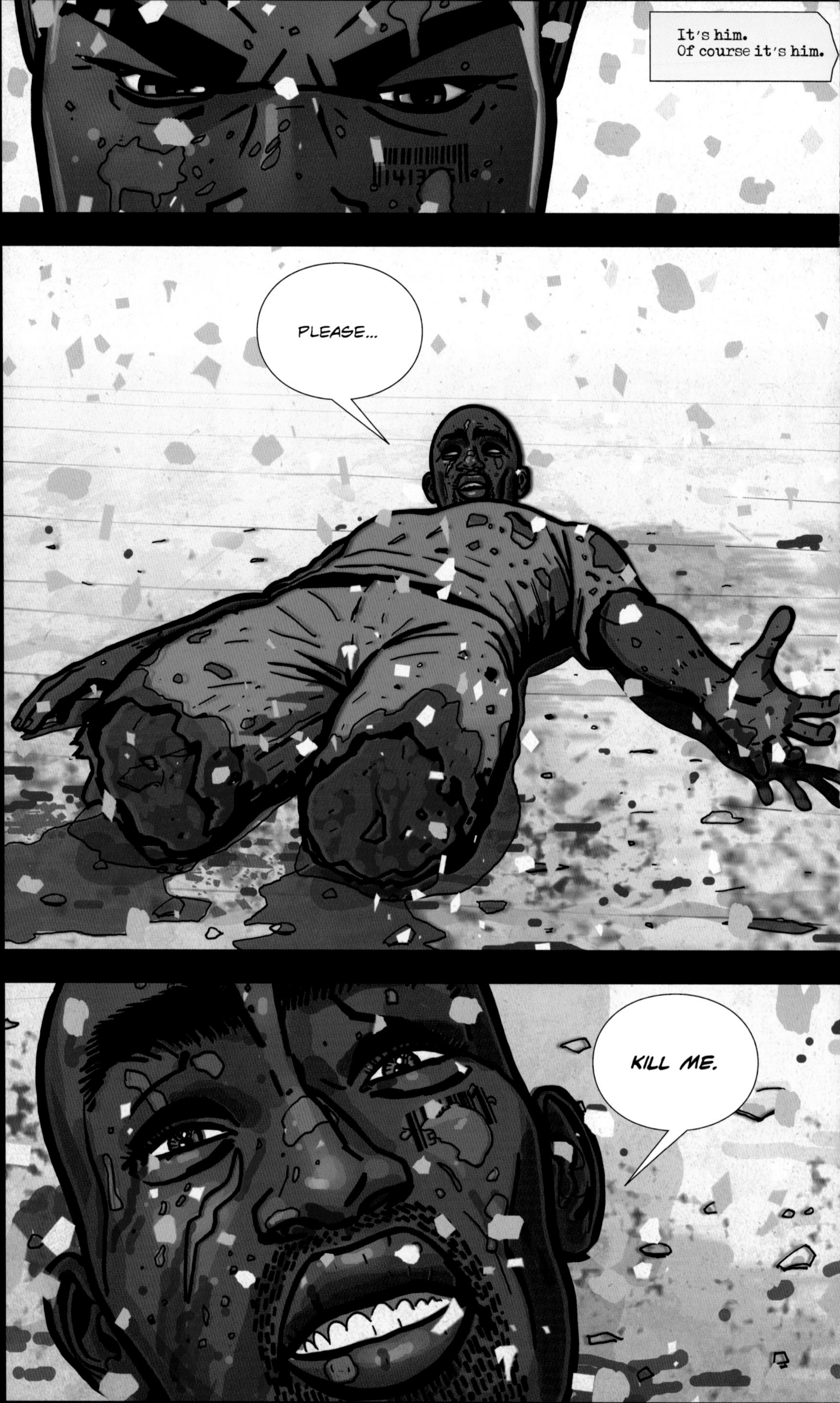
It's him.
Of course it's him.
PLEASE...
KILL ME.

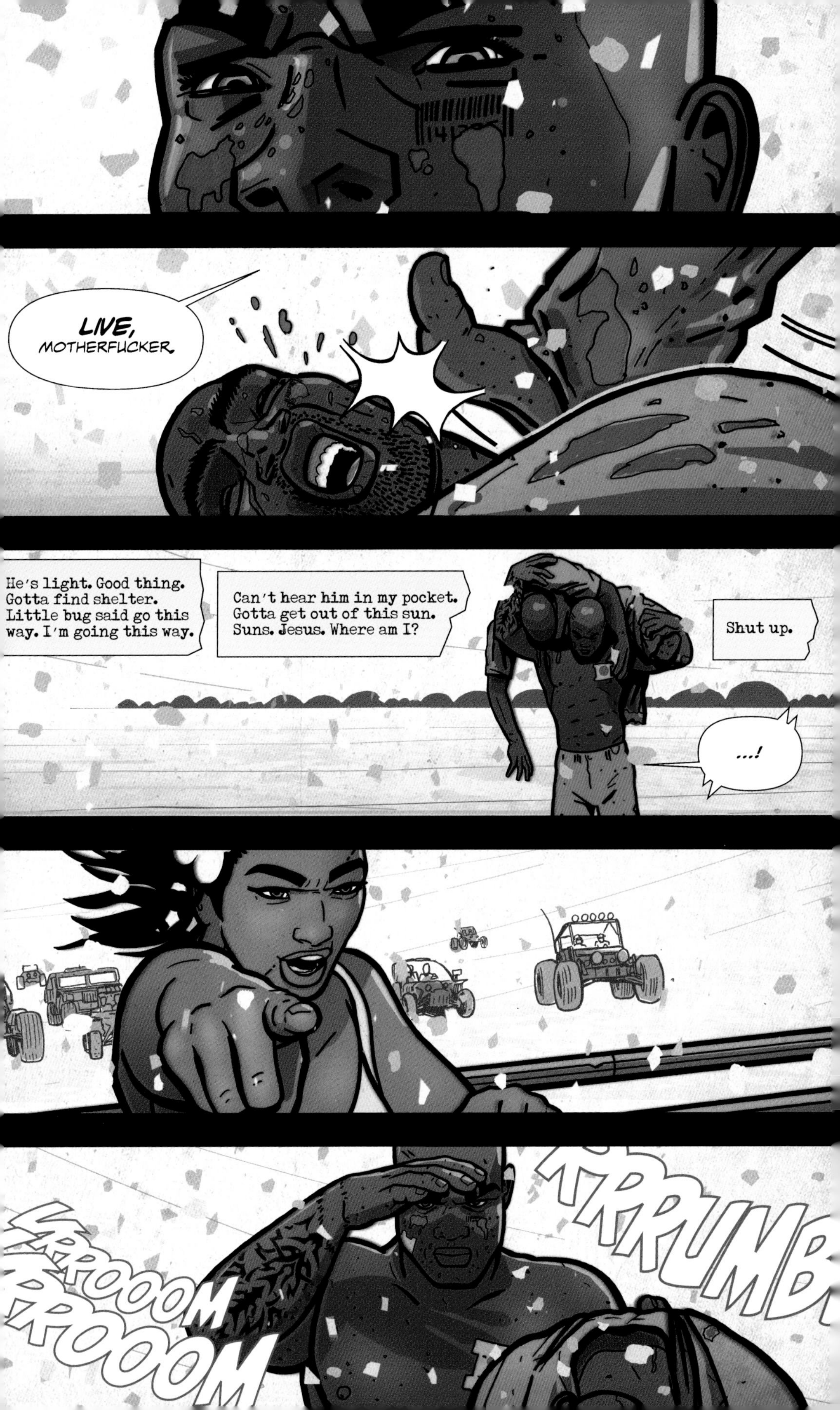

LIVE, MOTHERFUCKER.
He's light. Good thing. Gotta find shelter. Little bug said go this way. I'm going this way.
Can't hear him in my pocket. Gotta get out of this sun. Suns. Jesus. Where am I?
Shut up.
...!
VROOOOM VROOOM
KRRUMB

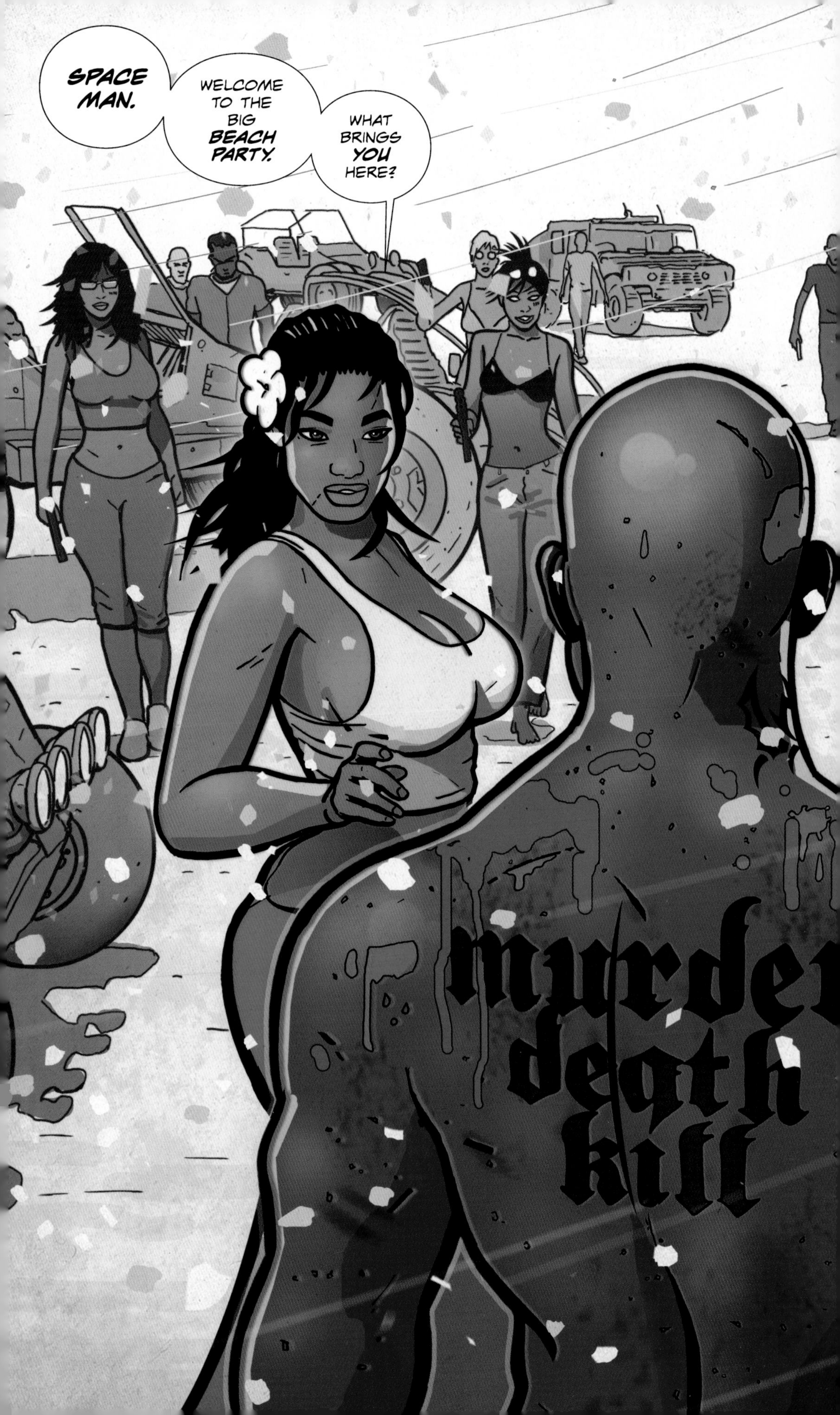
SPACE MAN.
WELCOME TO THE BIG BEACH PARTY.
WHAT BRINGS YOU HERE?
murder death kill

GLOSSARY

A GUIDE
TO THE GANGS
AND SLANG IN
CONCRETE PARK

THE GANGS OF SCARE CITY

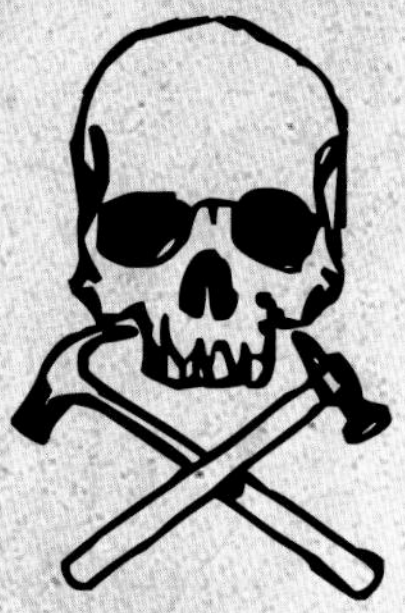

GIGANTE

Motto: "*Construimos.*" ("We Build.")

Gigante was the first gang—and is still the biggest gang—in Scare City. They have the sweetest deal with the NEC and they have the most powerful radio tower, which broadcasts the city's most popular station—Radio Gigante—thirty-two hours a day. Their unseen leader's name is Chavez. It's always Chavez. The name is titular, like *Kaiser*. The current Chavez, the seventh of that name, is the most unusual in this unusual line. He uses Radio Gigante as his pulpit, and on his daily show he broadcasts a radical call for peace in Scare City. As with so many other prophets of peace, a bad end for him is almost a foregone conclusion.

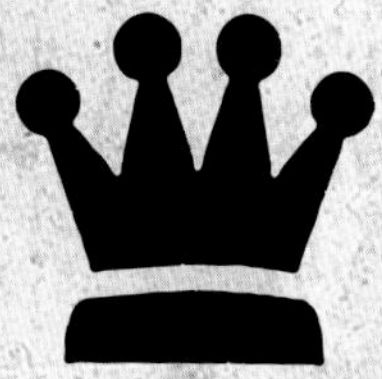

POTATO KING

Motto: "Famous Worldwide."

When he came to Oasis, he was a skinny but ambitious exile. His time in the mines made him tough and turned him into a leader. Today, at over eight hundred pounds, he is the biggest living thing on the surface of Oasis. Even in the planet's 0.9g, it takes two men to prop him up when he stands. He has cornered the market on alcohol in Scare City, and both he and the gang that follows him go by the name *Potato King*. Seeing his "King" label on a bottle of liquor means at least you won't die from the contents. Unless you want to. In a world where nothing grows, the Potato King has found a way to produce things that look, cook, and ferment like potatoes, an impressive and profitable achievement. He denies the rumors of cannibalism.

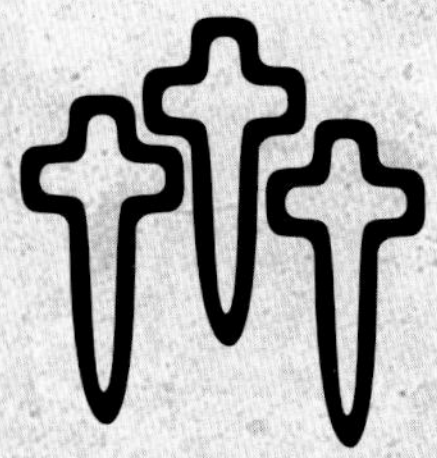

LAS CRUCES

Motto: "Three Sorrows."

Las Cruces is a mystery among the gangs of Scare City. The newest of the gangs, Las Cruces is building its strength through vigorous recruiting and aggressive business practices. "Aggressive business practices" means, in this context, murder. The leader of Las Cruces is a chain-smoking alien who only appears to be a human named Silas. He is actually one of the most powerful beings on the planet, a godlike spirit from when Oasis was young. What is his agenda? How many of his human cat's-paws must die before he gets what he's after?

M-80s

Motto: "Proof God Exists."

What little the Potato King doesn't own of the alcohol business in Scare City, the M-80s do. The M-80s' leader, Luca, is an old friend of the King . . . or she used to be. In these dangerous days, no one can say for sure who's safe. The M-80s is an all-woman outfit, a rarity among Scare City's gangs. From their tiny piece of turf in the Shoulder, they project a lot more power than their small numbers would warrant. That's because of Luca.

LOST HILL

Motto: "Don't Sleep."

Lost Hill is the second-largest gang in town. It's also in possession of the best strategic location, an enormous mesa at the edge of town from which they will never be dislodged. Their good fortune in having that location is also a curse, however. They have only so much room for growth. Thus, Lost Hill has a well-earned reputation for secretly initiating strategic partnerships with other gangs, only to betray them in the end, all with hopes of getting more "living room." Their motto, "Don't Sleep," is both a reminder of their own vigilance and an admonishment to all not to sleep on them.

BAMA

Motto: "Calamity."

More of a cult than a gang, Bama stands out as an insane, nihilistic group—even by the crazy standards of Scare City. Their leader, Fontaine, is a madman with a method, a paranoid visionary responsible for some of the darkest deeds ever done on Oasis. The gang lives in the desert, shunning the temptations of the city. Other gangs trade with the New Earth Council for money, influence, and power. Bama doesn't trade, doesn't want money, doesn't want influence, and doesn't want power. What, then, do they want?

According to NEC estimates, there are over one hundred other, smaller gangs, sets, and militias in Scare City.

CONCRETE PARK TERMS AND SLANG

A

ABDIDAS

n. A disparaging word encompassing all the fake-ass clothes and shoes made and sold on Oasis or brought used from Earth. *Also adj.* Fake, bogus, counterfeit.

B

BÁI MÙ

adj. Stupid. (Chinese, "white eyed, blind." On a desert planet with two suns and not enough sunglasses, this takes on a whole new meaning.)

BALLER

n. Someone who's got game.

BANGER

n. Gang soldier.

BAR 'N' GRILL

n. The identifying barcode mark of slavery tattooed on every exile's face.

BEM BOLADO

adj. Clever, cool. (Brazilian Portuguese, "well thought up.")

BHENCHOD

n. A contemptible person. In use all over the Indian subcontinent for eons, and in use now all over Scare City. Indians claim it; Pakistanis claim it. Wanna fight? Call someone *bhenchod*. (Hindi, "sister fucker.")

BIDI

n. A homemade cigarette. Silas smokes bidis. (Hindi.)

BINDASS

adj. Cool; carefree. A term of approbation, originally denoting a cool and carefree person, as in: "Check out my man Raj." "*Bindass.*" "*Bindass.*" Now, just an all-purpose word like cool that fits in any part of a sentence, as in: "See you." "*Bindass*, man, see you." (Hindi.)

BLUR

adj. Dense, stupid. As in the expression "*blur* like *sotong*" ("stupid as a squid"). (Malay.)

BRACE

v. To get arrested by the New Earth Council, resulting in injury or sometimes even death, as in, "A couple of bangers got braced last night. They won't be back." From the punning *NEC-brace*. See also **NEC-bone**.

BUMBACLOT

n. The king of curse words. (Jamaican, "ass wipe, ass cloth.")

C

CHARANGA

n. A loud-ass old car or truck. Also, a loud-ass gun. (Cuban Spanish, a type of dance band.)

CHEATERS

n. Sunglasses.

CHECKS AND BALANCES

n. The nine-foot-tall biomech cops of the New Earth Council. Part human, mostly machine, they once were gangsters. Injured, mutilated, arrested, the subjects of hideous medical experiments, they found themselves rebuilt into fearsome law-enforcement mechs.

CHOLA

n. A Latin gang girl, the female counterpart of a cholo. Arched eyebrows and gelled hair are a must. So is a razor. A chola is down for her barrio.

CHONGA

n. A gang girl with a Miami style, a somewhat less serious variant of a chola. If a chola is down for her barrio, a chonga is down for her hair gel and her barrio, in that order.

CINNABUN

n. A crazy person, mentally challenged. Also adj., as in, "This shit is cinnabun." (Anglo-Arabic, from Arabic *cinnadebun*, "to fly with the crazy eye.")

D

DAI LO

n. Big man, boss. Sometimes used sarcastically. (Cantonese slang.)

DALIT

n. An untouchable. On Oasis, the term takes in handicapped or differently abled people, outcasts within a world of outcasts. All parts-people could be considered Dalits, while not all Dalits are parts-people. (Hindi.)

DESAPARECIDOS

n. The missing. The exiles on Oasis. One of the hardest things for the exiles to accept is that successive waves of young humans have landed on this penal colony in space with no more knowledge of its existence than the first arrivals had, indicating that most people on Earth have no idea what the New Earth Council is doing or where huge numbers of Earth's poor youth are disappearing to. The young exiles are truly the forgotten ones. (Spanish.)

DESCANSO

n. A roadside marker or memorial to a victim of a shooting or an accident. (Spanish, "place of rest.")

DESI

n. A person from the Indian subcontinent, such as India, Pakistan, Bangladesh, or Sri Lanka.

DHIMMI

n. A second-class citizen; a little person; someone unaffiliated with a gang and therefore unprotected. (Arabic slang, from *ahl al-dhimma*, "people of the contract," the name for tolerated unbelievers in a Muslim state.)

DONNO GO WHERE

expr. Lost. (Malay pidgin, "I don't know where it went.")

E

EL EXILIO

n. The Exile. As in, "This is day whatever-the-fuck of El Exilio." Just as in prisons everywhere, most of the exiles on Oasis keep a running count of the days they've been there. The difference is there will be no parole; there will be no return home from El Exilio. (Spanish.)

EYEBORG

n. Biointeractive sunglasses with implants. Very helpful on sunny Oasis, very hard to come by. Also, synecdochic for people who wear these glasses and implants, as in, "What you lookin' at, eyeborg?"

F

FANAGALO

n. A pidgin miners' language based on Zulu, with English input, that spread from the mines of South Africa to the mines of Oasis.

FAVELA

n. A slum neighborhood; a barrio. See also **solar**. (Brazilian Portuguese.)

FIFTEEN

n. An AR-15, a much-prized assault rifle.

FILMI

adj. Looking like something out of a Bollywood movie, as in: "All new, all live filmi girls!" A term of art used to promote the charms of prostitutes. (Hindi.)

FRAUDBAND

n. NEC radio stations, which are notorious for broadcasting shit. Also, any bogus information.

G

GÀN NI MA

expr. "Fuck your mother." (Chinese.)

GA6

n. An outcast. It stands to reason a planet full of exiles would have multiple words in many languages for *exile, outcast, unwanted,* etc. Pronounced "gat." See also **olvidados, desaparecidos.** (Arabic.)

GAT

n. A gun.

GHORA

n. A gun. (Mumbaiya Hindi.)

GOD WINK

n. Something taken as evidence that a higher power is at work; a coincidence.

GUJU

n. A person from the Indian state of Gujarat who is good at business. *Also adj.* Admirable, as in, "You got him to pay what? Damn, son, that's *guju!*"

GULTI

n. A native speaker of Telugu from the Indian state of Andhra Pradesh, home to a subculture of engineers and software developers.

H

HACK-MECHA

n. A low-grade, improvised, or ad hoc prosthetic limb or other body part. *Also adj.* Used to describe a situation where the wiring is not up to code, as in, "That peace treaty won't last; it's just hack-mecha."

HANGER

n. A gang associate or second-class wannabe; a punk. See **banger**.

HOLEY

n. A friend or associate from the mines, a boon coon.

HOLEY-ER THAN THOU

expr. Used to describe someone who did more mine time than you, or someone who just cops that annoying, bullshit attitude.

HOPE ON A ROPE

n. Your ace holey. Someone who's absolutely got you. The friend who'll pull you up when you're down a cold, dark hole. (Miners' slang.)

HUDNA

n. A cease-fire. (Arabic.)

J

JHEELO

n. A zero. Someone who can do nothing, who has nothing, who is nothing; i.e., pretty much all the human exiles on Oasis. (Malay.)

JINETERA

n. A prostitute. (Spanish, "female jockey.")

K

KANJANI

expr. "How are you?" Common Fanagalo greeting among those who have served time in the mines; i.e., everyone in Scare City.

KEPLER 56-B
n. The original name of the planet Oasis. First identified (and immediately covered up) by German astronomers in 2007, it was named after the greatest of German astronomers. The existence of this (relatively) close, Earth-like world was kept secret for years. As evidence of vast ice deposits at the planet's poles mounted, a secret initiative was begun, complete with unmanned, and then manned, missions of exploration.

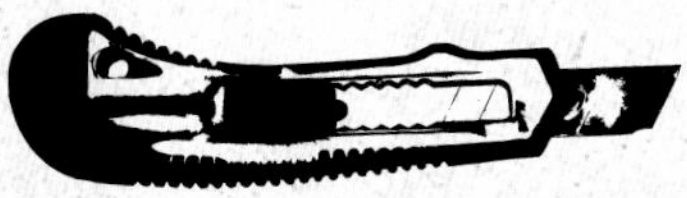

KIRK
n. The man, a badass, a stud, an interplanetary love god.

KOS SHE'R
n. Bullshit. (Farsi, "pussy poem.")

L

LOST AND FOUND
n. A church, mosque, temple, or place of worship.

LUPANGO
n. A slang name for the planet Oasis, originating with East African exiles. (Kiswahili, "prison.")

M

MADARCHOD
n. A despicable person. See also **bhenchod**. (Hindi, "motherfucker.")

MBUSHI
n. A derogatory term for someone living (or trying to live) in the desert wastes outside Scare City. (From Kiswahili *bushi*, "bush," someone too foolish to come in out of the wilderness.)

MIKEY
n. An untraceable phone. Often used as a proper noun, as in: "Who's calling?" "Mikey."

MOFONGO, THE BIG
n. Derogatory name for the Potato King, the Puerto Rican who, at 800+ pounds, is the biggest single living thing on the planet Oasis.

MOOK JUNG
n. A slow or stupid person. (Cantonese, "dummy," the wooden training dummy from a million kung fu films.)

N

NAAFI
n. A lazy person. (South African acronym, "no ambition and fuck-all interest.")

NEC-BONE
n. Human New Earth Council cops and workers. A despised group; collaborators; the lowest of the low. *Also v.* To arrest and maybe fuck someone up.

NEC-BRACE
v. To arrest and definitely fuck someone up all the way.

NEW EARTH COUNCIL
n. The human raj on Oasis. Shrouded in secrecy from its inception (at the time of the discovery of what was then known as Kepler 56-B, in 2007), the New Earth Council grew from a small initiative of the EU countries into a full-blown military government of the new world. The NEC has jurisdictional power to arrest, try, and transport anyone in the selected Earth demographic (young and poor). The NEC operates the massive ships that take the young human exiles on their two-year voyage to Oasis, and it directs all mining operations there.

O

OLVIDADOS
n. Forgotten ones. The human exiles on Oasis. (Spanish.)

P

PABLO
n. A drug dealer.

PARTS-PERSON

n. One with bionic or robotic implants or prostheses, from limbs to adrenaline pumps to hearts.

PATTY

n. Street money issued by an independent bank. Indie banks live and die on reputation, just as their Earth counterparts do, but without any sanction or backup from civil authorities. Also *hairy patty*. (Mumbaiya Hindi slang, *hari patti*, "green notes," as opposed to the red notes of the New Earth Council.)

PINCHE

adj. Fuckin', rotten, no-good, worthless, contemptible, nasty, filthy. The greatest all-purpose slang word on two planets. Thus *pinche puto*, "worthless fuck"; *pinche cabrón*, "no-good asshole"; etc. But on Oasis, *pinche* is used every day, all day, in the ubiquitous exile expression, "It's *pinche calor* today, holey" ("It's fuckin' hot") or just, "*Pinche calor.*" Everybody—black, white, Asian, bot, whatever—says this. (Mexican Spanish.)

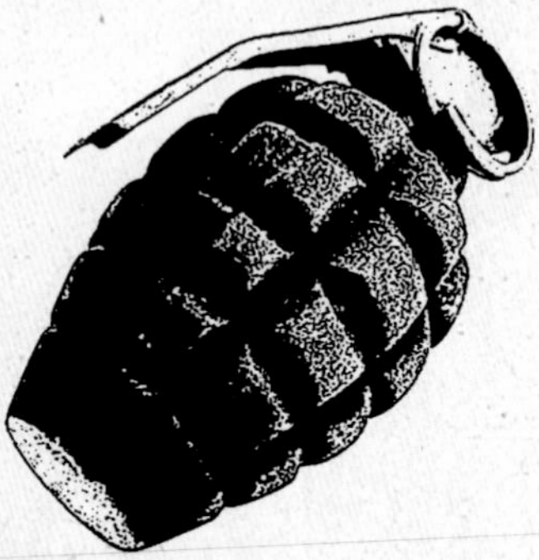

PROCIDIGAAADE

expr. Jargon, "Proceed to gate." For reasons that are unclear, many of the public-address announcers in the ice mines of Oasis are either Malays or have adopted their characteristic weary slur. Thus the announcement, "Lot 47, proceed to gate 12," becomes "Lah for-senn, procidigaaade twel-lah." In Scare City's twisted alleys and tangled favelas, street directions fall into this comical singsong: "Go up the hill, procidigaaade Sugar Street, left at the sign, procidigaaade ring-road . . ."

R

RANDI

n. A prostitute. Used as a proper name, it is a great insult, as in, "Shut up, Randi, nobody asked you shit." (Hindi.)

RED, REDS, RED BILLS, RED NOTES

n. New Earth Council–issued money.

S

SALAAMBRO

n. Arab.

SAMZDOT, SAM'S DOT

n. Forbidden information. Originally referred to forbidden digital information, but could be in any form. (From Russian *samizdat*.)

SANGOMA

n. Street healer, as opposed to a real doctor. (Zulu, Xhosa.)

SCARE CITY

n. The universal name for New Earth Correctional Colony City Number Two on the planet Oasis.

SMEAR

n. A cell culture, virus, or other bioactive building-block material for genetic design. What chips are to computing, smears are to life engineering.

SOLAR

n. A slum. (Brazilian Portuguese.)

SOTONG

n. A stupid person. (Malay, "squid" or "cuttlefish.")

SQUEEZE

n. The gang tax or surcharge on any transaction. You don't pay squeeze, you don't do business.

STEVE

n. A new arrival on Oasis; a rube; fresh meat. Everybody has been Steve at one time or another. The point is to not stay Steve. (Rhyming slang, "Steve Naive," from Steve Nieve, the Attraction.)

T

TAPORI
n. A street-smart kid. (Hindi.)

TSOTSI
n. Thug, gangster, no-gooder. A word which lent its name to a whole category of languages, *tsotsitaals* (mixed gangster creoles). The language of Scare City is growing into its very own *tsotsitaal*. (South African Sesotho.)

U

ULABU
n. A potent homemade beer primarily brewed and sold by Kenyans and other East Africans. You don't want to know what they make it with, but it does the job. *Also excl.*, as in (after knocking one back), "*Ulabu!*" (Kiswahili slang.)

X

XANA
n. Pussy. (Brazilian slang.)

XOTA, XOXOTA
n. See **xana**.

Y

YALLA-GANG
n. A small, unaffiliated kidnapping gang. (From Arabic, *Yalla, yalla!*, "Come on! Let's go! Hurry!")

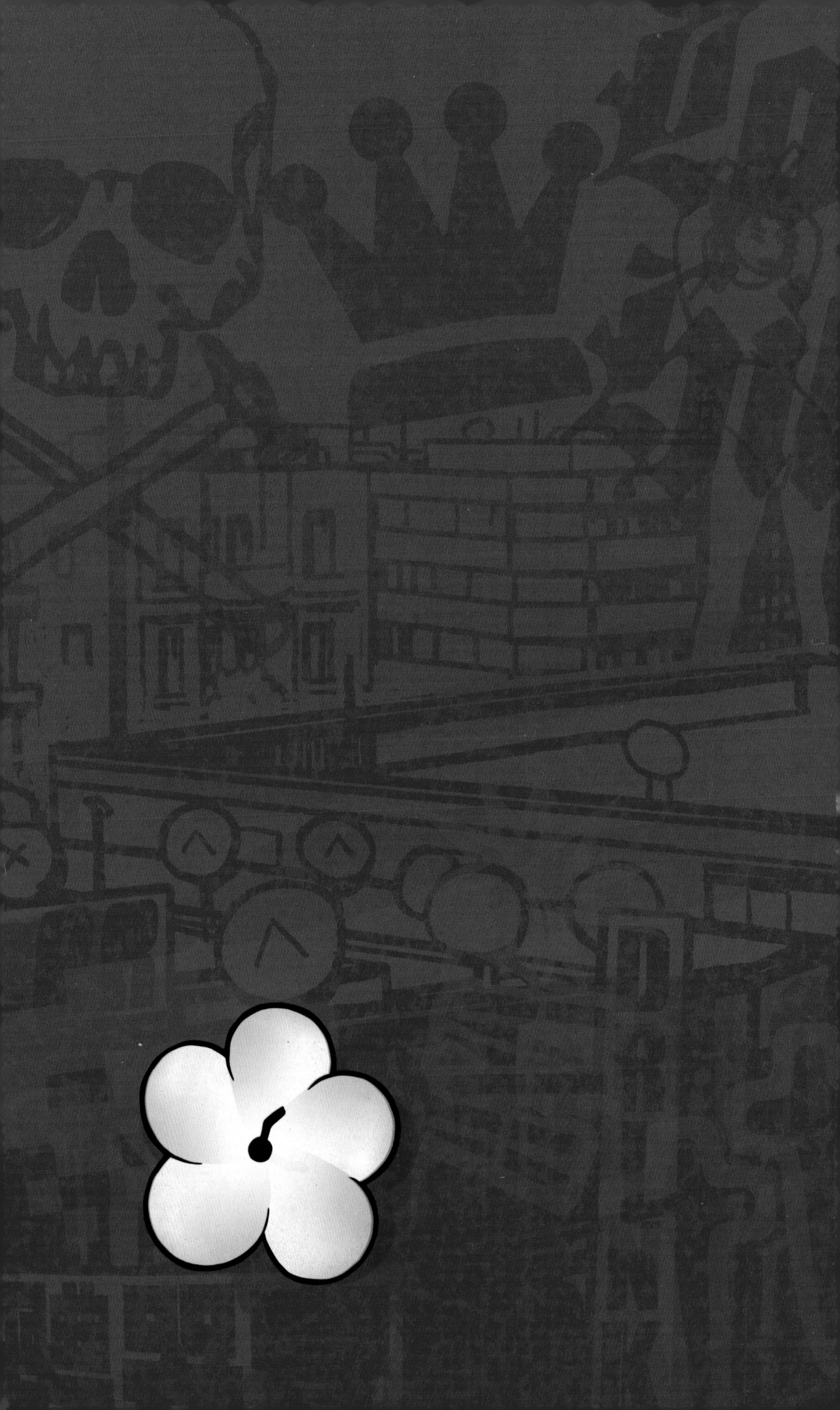

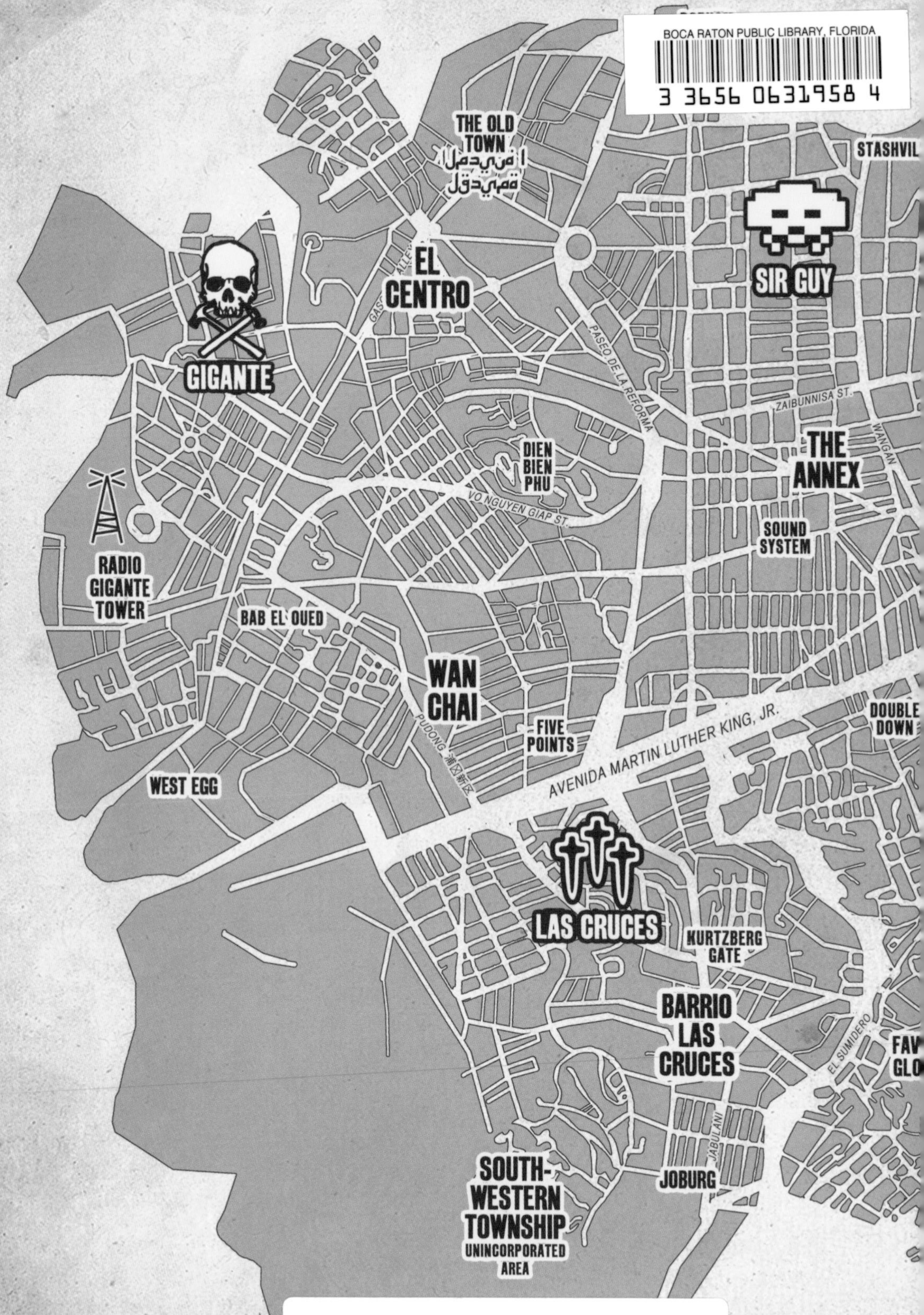
THE OLD TOWN
EL CENTRO
SIR GUY
STASHVIL
GIGANTE
PASEO DE LA REFORMA
ZAIBUNNISA ST.
WANGAN
THE ANNEX
DIEN BIEN PHU
VO NGUYEN GIAP ST.
SOUND SYSTEM
RADIO GIGANTE TOWER
BAB EL OUED
WAN CHAI
PUDONG
FIVE POINTS
DOUBLE DOWN
AVENIDA MARTIN LUTHER KING, JR.
WEST EGG
LAS CRUCES
KURTZBERG GATE
BARRIO LAS CRUCES
EL SUMIDERO
JABULANI
JOBURG
SOUTH-WESTERN TOWNSHIP
UNINCORPORATED AREA